YEAR-ROUND
GARDENING

D0707884

YEAR-ROUND
GARDENING

**Expert advice on
what to do in your garden
season by season**

Published by The Reader's Digest Association Limited
London ■ New York ■ Sydney ■ Montreal

CONTENTS

**MORAY COUNCIL
LIBRARIES &
INFO.SERVICES**

20 25 29 92

Askews	
635	

Summer

Autumn

Winter

Introduction

A garden can be a source of beauty, whatever the time of year. From the earliest bulbs of spring right through to winter-flowering shrubs, the joy of the seasons is in their variety.

There is something to enjoy in the garden all year round. When spring arrives and the days grow longer, a mass of different plants awake from their winter rest to transform the garden. The heat of summer encourages plants to put on a vibrant show and tender specimens come into their own. Autumn brings its own beauty with late-flowering perennials and the bold brightness of fading foliage. In winter there is still colour to be seen as some plants flower, but the chief interest is often the bare but colourful branches of trees and shrubs, and the sculptural forms of seedheads and grasses.

As the life-cycle of plants is regulated by the seasons, so is the gardener. The jobs you need to do in the garden depend on the time of year and it's important not to stray from the calendar too much. If, for example, you plant too early or too late you won't get the best display in the right season. Do the right job at the right time and you can ensure a beautiful looking garden all year round.

This book has four chapters, one for each season, each offering a guide to the important garden jobs that need to be done. For the purposes of this book, spring is taken as being March to May, summer is June to August, autumn is September to November and winter is December to February. The seasons, however, seldom stick to the calendar and will vary depending on where you live. You should, therefore, be guided by local conditions when planning your gardening year.

Spring

10 Perennials

With the first perennials already gracing the garden and routine maintenance underway, spring is an excellent time to propagate the next generation of herbaceous plants. These can be used to fill gaps in this summer's border or brought on for next year's display.

Spring checklist

■ **Weed, feed and mulch** established plants. Cut off any remaining dead growth and tidy up evergreens (see page 12).

■ **Lift and divide** established clumps of ornamental grasses and mid to late-summer flowering perennials and replant the divisions (see page 12).

■ **Repot container-grown plants** that are congested, and top-dress those remaining in pots with fertiliser and fresh compost.

■ **Plan new planting schemes** for your garden, then buy and plant new perennials and grasses while the weather conditions are still cool and moist. Look for well-established plants in large pots at the garden centre. These are a good buy as you can divide them up immediately into several smaller clumps (see page 14).

■ **Harden off plants** by removing winter protection once the weather has improved. Plants you have raised or overwintered under cover will need plenty of time to establish themselves before next winter (see page 15).

■ **Pot up young plants** that have developed from autumn or winter root cuttings and tender perennials overwintering under cover. Place them in fresh compost and water well to encourage new growth.

Hellebores offer a muted magnificence from late winter into spring. *Helleborus hybridus* 'Pluto' is hardy and clump forming.

Tidying a perennial border

1 Before applying a moisture-retaining mulch, remove perennial weeds such as tap-rooted dandelions and thistles.
2 To encourage strong new growth, cut out any dead and untidy stems from grasses and perennials.

■ **Protect new shoots** from slugs and snails, particularly those of susceptible plants such as delphiniums, hostas, lupins and peonies (see page 14).

■ **Take basal cuttings** from plants that produce an abundance of new shoots at ground level and insert them in cuttings compost to root (see page 13).

■ **Sow the seeds** of many perennial species, either those that you have bought or those you collected during the previous year (see page 12).

■ **Put supports or stakes in place** well before tall perennials reach the point at which they begin to flop over (see pages 15 and 60).

■ **Water thirsty young plants** that are still developing a root system if more than a few days go by without rain. Soft, leafy perennials that have just been planted need plenty of water to maintain their rapid pace of growth – in dry weather this means up to 5 litres (1 gallon) per week per plant.

■ **Mulch to reduce water loss** and suppress weeds. Cover the soil around plants with an organic mulch, such as composted bark, well-rotted manure or garden compost. Before you mulch, make sure the soil you intend to cover is thoroughly moist and clear of any perennial weeds. Then lay the mulch at least 7–8cm (3in) deep to keep the moisture in and to prevent sunlight from reaching the soil and thus stimulating weed seeds to germinate.

■ **Remove weeds regularly**, otherwise they will compete with your ornamental plants for food, space and moisture.

■ **Deal with aphids** as soon as they settle on the soft growth of perennials – vigilance is important. You can remove them by hand – gently wipe the aphids away with your fingertips, taking care not to damage the young shoots – or use an organic, oil-based spray that kills the pests as they feed.

■ **Lift and discard** some of the more invasive plants, such as creeping Jenny (*Lysimachia nummularia*).

■ **Encourage sideshoots to grow** from the base of new plants. Whether they have been raised from seed or from cuttings, make them bushier and stronger by removing the growing tip of each shoot, pinching between thumb and forefinger, once they reach a height of 10cm (4in).

As peony shoots emerge in spring their soft, tender growth is particularly susceptible to damage by slugs and snails. Protect as soon as new growth appears by covering with a cloche or use one of the various methods to eradicate slugs and snails (see page 15).

Sowing seed

This is the time to sow many perennials and grasses, which is an economical way of stocking a new garden or border. Certain varieties will even bloom this year if you sow them early and under cover. A few perennials need a period of cold in order to germinate. To achieve this, put the seed in a polythene bag with a little damp sand, and place it in the refrigerator for several weeks. Then sow in the following way:

■ **Sow seed in pots or trays** of moist seed compost, or direct into the soil in a coldframe or protected by a cloche.

■ **If sowing direct,** draw out shallow drills with a hoe and mix a little potting compost into the drill bottom to help retain moisture. Water the drill before sowing.

■ **Sow sparingly,** then cover with a thin layer of compost. Keep moist at all times.

■ **Once the seedlings** are big enough to handle, prick out into modular trays so each plant develops a compact root system.

Maintaining perennial beds

You need to prepare established perennials and grasses for the coming year before the plants start to grow rapidly and form new shoots. This new growth could be damaged by the work.

■ **First lift, divide and replant young,** vigorous portions of older perennials that have formed congested clumps.

■ **Lightly fork over the bare soil** between plants, mixing in a dressing of slow-release fertiliser at the same time.

■ **Remove all weeds,** particularly the roots of perennial ones, and closely inspect each clump of plants for weeds that may have taken root within the plant itself.

■ **Cut out to ground level** any dead stems that were not removed previously, and lift and discard some of the more invasive plants – such as creeping Jenny.

■ **Remove dead foliage** from evergreen grasses by combing carefully through the clump with your fingers. Also, cut off any tatty leaves from evergreen perennials such as bergenias.

■ **Mulch the bare soil** with a 5cm (2in) layer of organic matter, such as well-rotted manure, garden compost or chipped bark.

Dividing perennials

Lifting and dividing perennials in spring or autumn rejuvenates mature plants that have formed large, congested clumps. Wait for any that flower early, like bergenias, to finish blooming before you disturb them.

■ **Lift the clump** with a border fork when the soil is moist.

■ **Divide the clump** into pieces by pulling it apart, cutting it with a knife or using two forks back to back.

■ **Replant the young, outer sections** of the clump in the border. They will become established quickly.

■ **Discard the old central portion** and any sections carrying old flower stalks. They rarely produce any further flowers.

Dividing grasses

Well-established grasses in containers are a good buy as they can be divided into smaller clumps. These new plants will establish quickly and then spread out in the bed.

Taking a basal cutting

1 Many perennials produce abundant new shoots at ground level. Remove them from the base of the parent plant, using a sharp knife. Trim off any leaves from the bottom third of the cutting.

2 Next, dip the base of each cutting into a rooting hormone preparation. Take care to cover only the cut surface at the base of the cutting, as the rooting hormone may injure the stem.

3 Fill a pot to the rim with cuttings compost, ensuring that the surface is level with the rim. Do not press it down. Holding the cuttings vertically, insert them carefully into the compost so their bottom third is covered. Water gently.

Propagation

As new growth appears, it is time to take basal cuttings of a number of perennials, including achillea, anthemis, chrysanthemums, delphiniums, gypsophila and lupins. Sever the new shoots when they are 8–10cm (3–4in) high and insert them in a pot of cuttings compost; keep covered until they root.

Planting perennials

While many perennials can be planted in early spring or autumn, those with hollow stems are vulnerable to weather and must be planted in late spring. They include anchusa, delphiniums, euphorbias, hellebores, helianthus, kniphofias, liatris, phlox, ligularia, poppies (*Papaver orientale*),

Hostas, which offer attractive foliage and spikes of simple flowers, can be divided easily into smaller clumps. They are one of the few plants that will succeed on close-textured clay soils, although they do better if the ground has been improved with grit or organic matter, such as well-rotted garden compost.

Sedum spectabile and symphytum. If these perennials are planted out in autumn and made to spend their first few months sitting in cold, wet soil, rainwater can collect within their stems and cause them to rot. Once disease is introduced, it can spread quickly to the rest of the plant.

Before planting, dig the site thoroughly, removing all perennial weeds – such as thistles and dandelions – and incorporate some organic matter, such as well-rotted manure or garden compost. Allow the soil to settle for a week or two, then clear any remaining weeds and roughly rake the soil level before you begin planting out your new perennials.

Dig a planting hole large enough to accommodate the whole root system of the plant. When you take a bought-in plant from its container, remove the top 1cm (½in) of compost from the surface of the rootball before planting. This may contain weed seeds and moss that you would not want introduced to your garden.

The planting depth of perennials is critical. Most perennials have a shallow root system, with the body or crown of the plant either at or just below soil level.

■ **For perennials with fibrous root systems,** such as asters, carex and stachys, the top of the roots should be 1cm (½in) below the soil surface.

■ **Perennials with fleshier roots,** such as acanthus, bergenias and *Dicentra spectabilis*, need setting slightly deeper, at about 2–3cm (1in) below soil level.

■ **It is better to plant slightly too high** and then add more soil or mulch later on. If you plant too deeply there is a risk that the plant will rot in the ground.

TIP Buy an established perennial in a large pot rather than several smaller ones. When you get the plant home, remove it from the pot carefully and divide it into smaller pieces, each with several growing shoots and roots. These can then be planted out in the border as normal.

Planting perennials

1 Before planting out, water the container-grown plant thoroughly and leave it to drain. To remove it from its pot, support the stem and foliage, and then tap the container with your other hand.
2 Hold the plant by its rootball to position it in the hole at the correct depth. Pull the soil back around the plant and firm it gently into place.
3 Leave a slight depression round the base of the stem and water into this.

Dealing with slugs and snails

The new shoots of herbaceous perennials are soft and succulent and, being at soil level, make easy meals for slugs and snails. Try one of these methods to trap them:

■ **Hand-pick offenders,** particularly after rain and in the evening.

■ **Sink containers of beer** (or a 50:50 beer-and-water mix) in the ground; slugs and snails are attracted by the yeasty aroma, fall in and then drown.

- **Lay a grapefruit half** (flesh scooped out) near vulnerable plants. It will attract large numbers of slugs and snails, so check underneath each morning.
- **Grow leafy perennials in pots,** raised off the ground.
- **Lay slug pellets sparingly.** They are frequently used in far too great a quantity: 10 pellets per m² (1 per sq ft) should provide adequate control for one week.

Supporting perennials

Herbaceous perennials have soft, non-woody stems so when they reach a certain height they tend to flop. This can result in considerable damage to both stems and flowers, especially after rain when the blooms, heavy with water, cause the stems to keel over and collapse. Once a plant flops or is beaten down by rain it never recovers; however carefully you arrange its stems it will always look awkward.

Give extra support to tall-growing plants long before it is needed, and certainly before they have reached half their mature height. Ideally, the supports should be no more than two-thirds of the plants' ultimate height, so that their shoots and leaves grow through the supports and obscure them. Use any of the following:

- **Twiggy stems of birch or hazel,** known as brushwood, with the tips bent over.
- **Bamboo canes** (though these are more difficult to obscure).
- **Specially designed stakes** or supports that link together to form a frame around the plants as they develop; push these deep into the soil initially and ease them up as plants grow.

Hardening off

Perennials raised from seed can take two years from germination until they flower. If you sow in late summer or early autumn and grow plants under a coldframe, greenhouse or conservatory for the first winter, this period can be shortened.

Hostas have soft, succulent new shoots that are especially attractive to slugs and snails. As soon as the new growth emerges through the soil, it is essential to take precautions, otherwise the foliage will be shredded.

Perennials raised in this way, or propagated from root cuttings taken in late autumn or winter, will need to be acclimatised gradually to garden conditions. This is known as 'hardening off' and is done by standing the pots outdoors on warm, sunny days. Bring them under cover at night to protect them from cold and frost. This ensures that the plants will not suffer a serious check in their growth when they are eventually planted out.

Once the plants are fully acclimatised and the risk of heavy frost has diminished – this varies depending on where in the country you are – plant them out in the garden. With a full growing season ahead of them, they will be strong enough to survive outdoors throughout the following winter season.

TIP New perennials raised over winter and established plants that have been divided will be smaller in size than those bought at a garden centre, so plant them in groups of three or five of the same species. They will soon appear to merge into a single clump, making much more of a visual impact than if they were planted singly.

As the days lengthen, spring bedding transplanted in autumn will begin to flower. It is time to turn your attention to the summer display. Most annuals and bedding plants are sown now – indoors, in a greenhouse or outside in a prepared nursery bed – to ensure an abundance of flowers summer-long.

Spring checklist

■ **Sow tender bedding plants** and other half-hardy annuals under glass in early March (see page 18). Include plants such as nemesias, impatiens, petunias, nicotianas, gazanias and mesembryanthemums.

■ **Sow annual climbers** to make a good size by planting time. Cobaea, rhodochiton, thunbergia, morning glory, canary creeper and nasturtiums can all be started in small pots indoors in warmth (see page 30).

■ **Buy seedlings and plug plants** from garden centres, and pot up to grow indoors until planting time.

■ **Prick out seedlings** sown earlier, to give them more space to develop (see page 18).

■ **Protect all indoor sowings** and seedlings against damping off disease (see page 19).

Double daisies (*Bellis perennis*) form dense patches of long-lasting colour at the edge of a border if sown the previous spring.

■ **Plant out autumn-sown sweet peas** with suitable supports (see page 31). Move spring-sown plants to a coldframe, and sow a final batch in warmed soil where they are to flower.

■ **Remove cloches** and other frost protection from autumn-sown annuals, and thin seedlings if necessary. Lift thinnings carefully, without damaging the roots, using an old kitchen fork or seed label, and transplant (see page 19).

■ **Protect seedlings** from slugs and snails (see page 14).

■ **Dig or fork sites** for new flower beds. Ground dug in autumn can now be raked and levelled, ready to prepare seedbeds for outdoor sowing (see page 19).

■ **Begin transplanting** hardy annuals from their winter quarters to flowering positions; check seed packets for the correct spacing.

■ **Start sowing hardy annuals** outdoors at the end of March, or under glass if conditions are unsuitable for direct sowing.

■ **Harden off young plants** sown indoors earlier in spring that are nearly ready for planting out. Remove cloches and fleece from protected seedlings outdoors, and open cold frames on mild days to acclimatise young plants.

■ **Repot tender perennials** that have been overwintered under glass, such as pelargoniums and fuchsias, and water more freely to start into growth.

■ **Prick out and pot up** greenhouse seedlings to make large specimen plants, and plant out hardy annuals sown in spare ground last autumn.

■ **Buy summer bedding** at the garden centre and plant out (see page 20).

■ **Sow annuals** where they are to grow, especially those that dislike being transplanted. Do this from mid April to mid May in milder areas, two to three weeks later in colder parts of the country or where soils are slow to warm up.

■ **Sow biennials in drills outdoors** (see opposite) or start under glass for potting up or transplanting later.

■ **Grow a few annuals** for filling seasonal gaps later or for planting up pockets left in permanent displays; sow in rows in a vacant patch elsewhere in the garden, as for biennials, or sow under glass. Transplant the seedlings when large and robust enough to handle (see page 19).

■ **Weed regularly** between established annuals when the ground is dry and hoe lightly to loosen the surface of the soil.

■ **Collect seed** from your best spring annuals and biennials, and sow now or dry and store for later use.

■ **Sow a few pinches** of quick-growing annuals like candytuft (*Iberis*), california poppies (*Eschscholzia*) and love-in-a-mist (*Nigella*), where bulbs and early perennials are past their best, and also round spring-flowering shrubs for successional colour.

■ **Sow fast-growing** half-hardy annuals such as french marigolds (*Tagetes*), Mexican sunflower (*Tithonia*) and mallow (*Lavatera*) in the greenhouse.

■ **Take soft-tip cuttings** from vigorous plants of petunias, *Begonia semperflorens* and other tender annuals; choose non-flowering shoots or remove flower buds, and root the cuttings in a propagator or on a windowsill indoors.

■ **Sow the leftover seed** of taller annuals in rows at the side of vegetable beds, where they will provide a decorative edging and armfuls of flowers for cutting.

■ **Sow late-flowering annuals** such as asters, chrysanthemums and zinnias, either under glass or outdoors with protection from late frosts.

■ **Clear away any exhausted** spring bedding plants and prepare the ground for summer annuals.

Sowing biennials

1 Find a spare piece of ground that is out of sight but in good light and prepare a seedbed. Mark out straight, parallel drills 15–20cm (6–8in) apart in moistened soil. The seeds should be covered to double their depth in soil.

2 Using your finger and thumb, sprinkle the seeds thinly into the drill (do not sow straight from the packet). Cover them carefully and firm gently with the back of the rake.

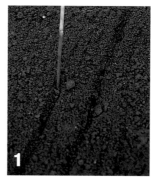 

Biennials for next spring

Forget-me-nots, wallflowers, sweet williams and foxgloves all need to make plenty of growth this season so that they overwinter outdoors successfully and flower prolifically next year.

Sow them outdoors in drills in a nursery bed or vacant piece of ground during late spring (see above). Ensure that they are in a bed that will get plenty of light. Cover the bed with netting if you think that birds, squirrels or cats are likely to damage the emerging plants.

When the seedlings are large enough to handle, thin to about 5cm (2in) apart. About two weeks later, thin them again, this time ensuring that smaller varieties are spaced 10cm (4in) apart and larger ones 15–20cm (6–8in) apart.

Water as needed and feed once or twice in summer. In autumn, lift plants with a trowel and transfer them to the beds or containers where they are to flower next spring.

Pricking out seedlings

1 Use the forked end of a dibber or the point of a seed label to ease a cluster of seedlings out of the pot. Make sure the compost is moist before attempting this. Then separate the seedlings gently and spread them out on a board.

2 Once you have filled a seed tray with compost, mark four rows and make six holes about 5cm (2in) apart. Seedlings are delicate and their fragile stems easily crushed, so handle them by their leaves when inserting into a hole, then gently firm.

3 When all the seedlings are in position, water the tray using a watering can with a fine rose and then label it. Position the tray in a well-lit place but keep the seedlings out of direct sunlight. Plant out when the leaves are touching each other.

Raising annuals under glass

Half-hardy annuals cannot stand frost. They are always sown under glass because if you wait until conditions are warm enough to sow outdoors, the plants will flower very late. Most can be sown now, but some need a long growing season, and antirrhinums, pelargoniums and *Begonia semperflorens* are best sown in late winter if they are to make substantial plants in time for planting out as bedding.

For successful germination you need to provide an ambient temperature of about 18°C (64°F) in a greenhouse or propagator. If it is not possible to do this, wait until March when artificial heating to 10°C (50°F), combined with increased sunlight, should still ensure success.

Where an unheated greenhouse or coldframe is the only aid available, buy temperature-sensitive plants such as begonias, lobelia and petunias as seedlings or plugs, and concentrate on sowing more robust, faster-growing tender annuals like china asters, nemesia, *Tagetes* and zinnias in April.

Lack of heat is no handicap to growing hardy annuals. These plants are normally sown direct outdoors, but they may also be started indoors without artificial heat in early March to provide strong, branching plants for transplanting outdoors in late April or May. Use this method to raise superior plants of calendulas, clary, dimorphotheca, lavatera, nasturtiums and larkspur for containers and greenhouse pot plants, and for filling gaps in borders.

The importance of thinning

Most annuals germinate quickly if sown in the right conditions, and *Tagetes*, annual chrysanthemums and zinnias emerge less than a week after sowing. They soon develop into dense clusters of seedlings, all struggling for light and becoming spindly. These are ideal conditions for the spread of damping-off disease – this is caused by a range of virulent, soil-borne fungi that can rapidly destroy an entire tray of seedlings.

To avoid early overcrowding, sow seeds as sparingly as possible. Prick out or thin seedlings as soon as they are ready, to ensure that they have space to grow strongly and avoid the soft, leggy growth and matted roots that result from overcrowding.

Pricking out

By the end of February, some of the earliest seedlings should have one or two true leaves above the initial pair of seed leaves, and will be large enough to handle comfortably. Prick them out into trays, preferably modular ones of 6, 9 or 12 compartments, which gives them room to develop individually, or space them out in plain seed trays (see left). Pot up larger seedlings individually in 6–8cm (2½–3in) pots.

Sowing annuals direct

Many half-hardy annuals make the strongest and bushiest plants if sown initially under glass. However, for large displays this is laborious so it is often better to sow directly in the ground in late March or April.

Prepare the ground as soon as it is workable by forking the soil one spade blade deep where it has not been cultivated since last autumn. Sites that have already been dug over should need only light forking to break up the surface and any large clods.

Rake to level and to leave a fine tilth ready for sowing. You can protect this seedbed from heavy rain or prolonged dry weather by covering it with a plastic sheet weighted down with bricks, or with a portable coldframe. This will also warm the soil and, after two to three weeks, you can sow seeds you have bought or saved from last year with a good chance of rapid germination.

Annual grasses

Most annual grasses are easy to grow and produce graceful, airy plants for garden display and also for drying. They tend to mature quickly, rather than last the whole season, but you can avoid an untidy appearance in late summer by cutting off the dry seed heads for indoor use, clearing plants and replacing them with late-flowering annuals or more grasses from a later sowing made in June.

- **Sow and keep indoors** in 8cm (3in) pots during March, because seedling grasses are hard to distinguish from weed grasses.
- **Grow a few seeds in each pot** and thin them out if necessary to leave several evenly spaced seedlings.
- **Harden off and plant out** in late May or early June for tender species such as sorghum.
- **Plant in bold groups,** or thread the grasses between other bedding for maximum effect.
- **Cut for drying** just before seeds are ripe, as they shed easily, and hang up in a warm, airy place.

Fox-tail barley (*Hordeum jubatum*) has dense panicles of light green spikelets displaying impressive bristles that are tinted red or purple before turning beige.

BEDDING SCHEMES

Plants for bedding may be hardy or half-hardy annuals, biennials, bulbs or tender perennials, according to the season in which they flower. Spring bedding is normally composed of bulbs such as daffodils, tulips and hyacinths, planted in autumn together with biennials like wallflowers, pansies and forget-me-nots, then dug up when flowering ceases. Summer bedding uses hardy and half-hardy annuals, often blended with tender perennials such as pelargoniums and fuchsias, and carries the display from the end of the spring bedding season through to the autumn, when cleared plants are replaced with spring bedding.

Bedding styles

Formal bedding is set out in a geometrical pattern, with taller varieties ('dot' plants) at the back or in the centre, and the smallest plants along the edges. The space between is filled with mid-height plants, grouped in a mosaic of repeated shapes (see opposite).

Informal bedding dispenses with the geometry of straight lines and patterns, setting out the plants in relaxed groups that may overlap and even flower at different times to produce a more natural effect. A version of the herbaceous border, this often uses hardy and native annuals rather than tender bedding plants.

Colour schemes

There are no firm rules about colour combinations; you could blend a few complementary shades in a subtle design, or mix a whole rainbow of contrasting colours. Reds and oranges have a hot impact, while blue, mauve and white are tranquil. Leaves can be as colourful as flowers, and foliage plants such as coleus, silver senecio and golden helichrysum make a great choice.

Raising the plants

Even a small bed can hold a surprisingly large number of plants. You need to decide whether to buy bedding as young plants or to grow from seed – a much cheaper option but dependent on having a greenhouse or space on a warm windowsill.

Popular annuals and tender perennials are usually offered by garden centres as seedlings or plug plants early in the season, or as larger plants in bud or flower a few weeks later. A much wider range is available if you grow from seed. Start 12–16 weeks before you need to plant out – spring bedding in mid-autumn and summer bedding after the last spring frosts. Half-hardy annuals will need heat for germination and early growth. The most successful are F1 hybrids, which produce uniform plants with large, bright flowers.

Bedding-scheme guidelines

- Select an open, sunny site for your scheme that offers plants shelter from strong winds, especially if you include tall central 'dot' plants over 60cm (2ft) high, such as cordylines or cannas.
- Keep the design bold and simple. In large beds, use big blocks of plants as smaller ones can look too fussy.
- Before planting out, make sure plants have been hardened off and water them.
- Start by positioning dot plants in the centre, spacing them 1m (3ft) apart. Use canes to support them if necessary.
- Use edging plants to frame the bed, placing them 15cm (6in) from the sides and 10–15cm (4–6in) apart, according to size and vigour.
- Fill in the spaces with medium-height flowers spaced 23–30cm (9–12in) apart.

Sowing a hardy annual bed

1 Remove weeds and then rake the soil to leave a fine tilth. Use dry sand and trickle it onto the ground to mark out an informal shape for each variety.

2 Draw out shallow lines or drills within each section, using a trowel. Use a stick as a guide.

3 Using your thumb and finger, sow seed thinly in each drill. Cover with a little soil, and firm down using the back of a rake. After a few weeks, remove weed seedlings by hand and thin annual seedlings as necessary (see page 19).

Purple, pink and white *Salvia viridis* and pink lavatera form colourful drifts. Hardy annuals look best in informal groups in a border.

Maintaining a scheme

Water the bed thoroughly immediately after planting, and repeat every seven days if rainfall is light. Keep the ground weed free by hoeing and then by hand weeding when the bedding plants have filled out. A mulch of lawn garden compost will help suppress weeds and keep the soil moist. Give plants a high-potash feed at midsummer and repeat monthly to keep them in peak condition. Prolong flowering by deadheading.

At the end of each season, remove tired plants and prepare the ground for the next display. Dig up and dry bulbs after spring bedding and discard herbaceous flowers. Remove weeds, tidy the edges, spread a dressing of general fertiliser and rake the surface. In mid-autumn, clear the bed of summer plants. Compost the annuals after saving any seed and transfer tender perennials to a greenhouse. Fork in a 5cm (2in) layer of garden compost and level.

Bulbs are a wonderful way of bringing colour to the garden in early spring and with a little effort now you can ensure they thrive year after year. But bulbs need not be exclusively for spring: tender or more exotic species can be planted now, ready to take starring roles in the summer border.

Spring checklist

■ **Check summer bulbs** that have been stored over winter to ensure that they are still in good condition; discard any poor or damaged specimens. Make plans for planting them in batches for extended summer flowering (see page 24).

■ **Bring indoors** the last potted spring bulbs and keep in a cool, well-lit place until buds show colour.

■ **Move or divide clumps of snowdrops** and winter aconites while they are still in leaf (see page 25).

■ **Buy snowdrops** 'in the green', that is with their foliage still in place, and plant out.

■ **Plant lilies outdoors** in borders or pots. You can transplant lilies by digging them up with large, undisturbed rootballs while the stems are still short.

■ **Feed bulbs naturalised in lawns** in March, and those in pots and borders after flowering (see pages 23–4).

■ **Sprout gladioli corms under glass.** Press them into a tray of compost and keep them moist and warm, then plant them out in March together with some dormant corms. These will bloom two to three weeks later to continue the display.

■ **Take dahlia cuttings** from tubers sprouted in winter, and start more tubers into growth (see page 24).

■ **Mark the position** of outdoor bulbs that might need moving.

■ **Plant summer-flowering bulbs** in mild gardens (see page 24).

■ **Pot up begonias, ranunculus** and other bulbs in coldframes and unheated greenhouses for flowering indoors.

■ **Pot or repot** tender bulbs such as vallotas and clivias, together with a last batch of amaryllis.

Deadheading

1 Daffodils should be deadheaded singly as their flowers fade and die.

2 Hyacinths must have the small blooms stripped off individually because the stem continues to manufacture food in the same way as the leaves.

The importance of leaving bulb foliage

A bulb can be badly weakened if its leaves are removed too early as they act as its food factory. Early removal can prevent a bulb from flowering the following year and, over several years, bulbs will die if foliage is tidied excessively. Foliage should not be knotted or cut off until it starts to yellow about six weeks after flowering. If dying foliage spoils the appearance of a border, sprinkle seeds of a fast-growing annual, such as nigella, around the leaves to hide them.

■ **Plant dahlias and begonias** as dormant or sprouted tubers (see page 24). Fork the ground deeply and work in plenty of rotted manure or garden compost; just before planting apply a top dressing of balanced fertiliser at 125g per sq m (4oz per sq yd).

■ **Cut large begonia tubers** into sections. Ensure each piece has at least one bud and plant as normal.

■ **Plant *Anemone coronaria*** in April for flowers in August.

■ **Plant a batch of gladioli** every two weeks until late May for a succession of blooms.

■ **Plant lily bulblets** and gladiolus cormlets, saved in autumn, in pots or nursery rows to flower in a year or two.

■ **Mark dense clumps of spring bulbs** that did not flower well. They are probably overcrowded and should be dug up and divided later in the year.

■ **Bright red lily beetles** and their orange-black grubs must be removed from lily plants by hand or sprayed with permethrin.

■ **Tie tall stems** of lilies, galtonias and gladioli to canes, if your garden is windy.

■ **Deadhead bulbs** as flowers fade so they conserve energy.

■ **When flowering is finished** leave the foliage of spring bulbs undisturbed. Conceal dying leaves with other plants (see above).

■ **Feed spring bulbs** with high-potash fertiliser after flowering.

■ **Sow seeds of summer bulbs** in seed trays in a cold frame.

■ **Rake soil over holes** left by dead bulb leaves to deter narcissus flies.

Indoor bulbs after flowering

Cut off dead flowerheads and stand indoor bulbs, in their pots or bowls, in an unheated room or a coldframe. Continue to water and feed them with a high-potash liquid fertiliser. In March, harden them off for a few days, then plant the contents intact in the ground where the foliage can die down naturally. Let the bulbs flower normally next year, but lift them again for forcing the year after.

Bulbs in lawns

Naturalised bulbs such as narcissi, crocuses and fritillaries can compete comfortably with the grass in a lawn, provided you do not feed that area with a lawn fertiliser. The high nitrogen content will boost the growth of the grass more than that of the bulbs. Instead, feed the bulbs as they appear in early spring with a light watering of high-potash liquid fertiliser or a sprinkling of bone meal, which will benefit the bulbs without stimulating grass growth.

Dividing aconites

Like snowdrops, winter aconites are best divided and transplanted 'in the green', before their leaves die down (see opposite).

Soft-tip dahlia cuttings

One of the easiest ways to propagate dahlias is to take soft-tip cuttings in spring and root them in gentle heat. Start in early spring by checking the tubers and cleanly cutting off any withered sections before burying them in trays of moist compost.

- **Space the tubers** so that they sit on a shallow layer of compost in the trays and heap more compost around them until the lower half is buried; water once thoroughly.
- **Keep in a warm, well-lit position** as the buds break and develop into new shoots.
- **Sever the shoots** just below the lowest leaf when about 5–8cm (2–3in) long, and root in a propagator.
- **Let the parent plant continue to grow** until late spring, when it can be planted outdoors or potted up in a deep, 10–13cm (4–5in) container.

Summer bulbs

Most summer bulbs are planted from late April onwards, but it is worth starting a few earlier in mild gardens and warm, sheltered positions. Suitable bulbs include brodiaea, eucomis, galtonia, sparaxis, tigridia and tritonia. Make sure the site gets full sun and drains freely; in heavy soils, bed the bulbs on a 5cm (2in) layer of grit and plant 8–10cm (3–4in) deep.

Whereas spring bulbs make the greatest impact massed in large colonies or naturalised drifts, summer bulbs and tubers look more effective in small, strategic groups. Plant them to provide localised, colourful highlights in flower borders as well as to rectify any midsummer gaps in beds and borders that have been left by earlier flowering perennials.

There are many summer-flowering bulbs and tubers to fit the bill. Tigridias and butterfly gladioli are useful 'dot' plants, or high points, or are good for cutting; begonias, cannas and dahlias create hot spots of lively colour; some lilies have a wonderful scent; and, galtonias and crinums make stately plants that contrast strikingly with the softer, rounded shapes of many herbaceous perennials.

- **For containers,** use a trowel or bulb planter and plant most of these bulbs at twice their depth in a pot of rich, soil-based compost. Make sure you include some

Planting dahlias

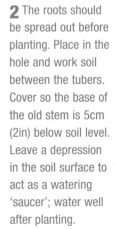

1 Dig a hole wide enough for the tubers and about 15cm (6in) deep. By placing the rootball in the hole, you can check the depth. For tall-growing varieties drive in a 1m (3ft) cane off-centre.

2 The roots should be spread out before planting. Place in the hole and work soil between the tubers. Cover so the base of the old stem is 5cm (2in) below soil level. Leave a depression in the soil surface to act as a watering 'saucer'; water well after planting.

Dividing winter aconites

1 Shortly after they have flowered, fork up a dense clump of established aconites. These can then be transported to a different part of the garden.

2 By teasing the clump apart it is possible to separate individual tubers or small clusters, which will allow you to select the number of plants required.

3 Use a narrow trowel to open up small holes in fresh ground or in the lawn if you want them to grow through grass. The holes should be spaced 15cm (6in) apart. Replant a tuber in each hole, making sure it is deep enough to bury the white portion of stem. Tread gently to firm all round.

crocks at the bottom of the pots for drainage. Then stand containers outdoors, feed regularly from six weeks after potting and avoid over-watering.

■ **With large bulbs like lilies,** plant three or five (odd numbers tend to look better) halfway down a 25–30cm (10–12in) container. These can then be used to brighten the summer patio or to plunge into borders where gaps occur.

■ **Plant begonias, cannas and dahlias** as dormant tubers about six weeks before the last frosts are expected for your locality. Space them 60cm–1.2m (2–4ft) apart, according to the size they are expected to grow.

■ **If you took dahlia cuttings** in early spring (see opposite) or set the tubers to sprout, plant them out once the threat of frost has passed.

Crocosmias create a striking splash of vibrant colour in the late summer border; *Crocosmia* 'Lucifer' has fiery red flowers. Also known as montbretia, they grow quickly and soon form large clumps that are ideal positioned between shrubs.

Pruning is essential in early spring to ensure strong growth, shapely bushes and masses of blooms throughout the season. Keep watch for early signs of pests and diseases, too. By late spring, roses will be sprouting fresh foliage and new shoots, with the earliest blooms appearing by the end of May.

Spring checklist

■ **Bare-rooted roses** can still be planted out at this time, provided you complete the process by early April.

■ **Continue planting** container-grown roses. They will benefit from being well established before midsummer.

■ **Tidy rose beds,** clearing away any fallen leaves and other winter debris.

■ **Trim and tidy ground cover** and edging plants growing in rose beds and borders.

■ **Check climbers and ramblers** to ensure that they are securely tied in. Make sure the supports are in good repair and that ties are secure but not too tight.

■ **Mist roses grown in pots under glass** with water occasionally to stimulate new growth and deter red spider mite. Keep the plants at a temperature of about 10–15°C (50–60°F) to encourage an early show of flowers. Watch out for pests and diseases, and feed at every other watering once new growth appears.

■ **Cut out any dead and damaged wood** from roses early in the season, in preparation for pruning.

■ **Sow rose seeds** taken from hips that have been exposed to cold over winter in pots of soil-based compost. Germinate in a warm place and then pot on and stand in a coldframe or cool greenhouse.

■ **Gently refirm roses** in the soil if frost has lifted their roots.

■ **Remove winter protection** from young and newly planted roses.

■ **Prune climbing roses** if they were not done in late winter. (Ramblers are pruned in summer.)

■ **Shorten some of the oldest** and thickest stems of climbing roses by half their length, to stimulate new main branches to appear lower down (see page 29).

■ **Start pruning other roses** beginning with shrub roses (see page 29).

■ **Protect bushes with wire guards** in areas where rabbits are a problem; keep the

Successful pruning will ensure that rose bushes and climbers produce strong, healthy red-tinged early shoots. But watch out for greenfly, which can severely damage new growth.

guards in place until buds have opened into strong new shoots.

■ **In a mild season,** feed pruned roses in late March with a balanced dry fertiliser or special rose feed (see page 74), and hoe or rake into the soil surface.

■ **Watch out for pests and diseases;** the first signs of blackspot, mildew and greenfly can appear as early as February if the weather is warm. Treat immediately to prevent serious infestation.

■ **Start weeding** between rose plants during mild spells.

■ **Finish pruning,** especially if spring is frosty and late, but try to complete this by mid-April at the latest.

■ **Hoe round established plants** regularly to deter weeds and keep bare soil loose and crumbly; hoe only the top 2–5cm (1–2in) of soil to avoid damage to rose roots. Deeper weeds should be hand-pulled or carefully dug out with a trowel.

■ **Moss and green slime** on the ground are indicators of soil compaction, which is especially common after a wet winter and spring. This can be remedied by shallow forking and hoeing.

■ **Feed roses** with a powdered or granular feed once spring pruning is finished, and again in midsummer.

■ **Give a foliar feed** where soil is poor or plants are ailing. Repeat this at monthly intervals up to the end of July.

■ **Mulch roses** as soon as the ground warms up in May and again after feeding.

■ **Plant ground cover** and edging perennials in rose beds.

■ **Check stakes, supports and ties** on climbing, rambler and standard roses, and loosen or renew them where they are worn or too tight (see above).

■ **Start disbudding hybrid tea roses** grown for top-quality blooms by rubbing or pinching out all but the main bud at the end of each shoot.

■ **Inspect the new growth on bushes** and standards for overcrowded or inward-

Tie in the new stems of climbers

New stems on climbing and rambler roses need to be spaced out. Use soft garden string to secure vigorous stems to their supports. To promote flowering, it is best to arch the stems sideways on walls and trellis, and spiral them around vertical posts. This is also a good opportunity to remove one or two of the oldest branches and replace them with new stems.

growing shoots, and pinch them out at their base or at a low bud.

■ **Check the watering needs** of roses being grown under glass daily as they come into flower. Give them a liquid feed every 10–14 days. Watch out for health problems, including red spider mites. Ventilate freely and shade the glass to keep temperatures down. When flowering has finished, stand the pots outside.

■ **Water roses planted in early spring,** especially during prolonged periods of dry weather.

■ **Sow miniature roses** in warmth under glass in April. As seeds germinate erratically, sow them thinly in a large seed tray and prick out the individual seedlings when they are large enough.

Pruning

Roses must be pruned annually to prevent them turning into shapeless, tangled shrubs with few flowers. Pruning should usually be carried out in mid-March in the south and west of the British Isles; in late March in central areas; but not until April in northern gardens and those on high or exposed ground. The danger of pruning too early is that buds are stimulated into life and may then be injured by hard frosts. Pruning late, when the sap is rising, means you cut off growing shoots, wasting the plant's energy and exposing open wounds to disease.

Identifying rose types

Different types of rose require individual pruning to achieve the best results.

■ **Hybrid teas** have long, sturdy stems with flushes of large shapely blooms borne singly or in small groups at the ends of sideshoots. **Pruning:** limit the main stems to about five per bush, and shorten these to four or five buds from the base – or just two buds for extra vigour and fewer, superior flowers.

■ **Floribundas** bear smaller flowers in clusters or sprays on freely branching bushes throughout the season. Patio roses are compact, bushy floribundas that seldom exceed 60cm (2ft) in height, with trusses of proportionately smaller flowers. **Pruning:** keep five or six stems on each plant, and prune older stems to five or seven buds long; lightly trim young new shoots or leave them unpruned.

■ **Shrub roses** are a varied group. Some old roses, like rugosas and centifolias, may bloom only once a year, whereas modern shrub roses are repeat flowerers and vary from dainty bushes to virtual climbers. **Pruning:** lightly prune to shape, thin any overcrowded shoots, and cut one or two of the oldest branches to ground level or a low sideshoot to stimulate new growth.

■ **Ground-cover roses** are a kind of shrub rose with low, dense, spreading growth that can cover large areas.

Shearing roses

Some gardeners prefer this less time-consuming approach to rose pruning, and trials have shown that simply shearing off excess growth is just as effective as the traditional rose pruning methods. Shearing is done at the same time as pruning, using garden shears, secateurs or a hedge trimmer. Cut bushes down to about half their height, leaving the weaker, twiggy growth unthinned but removing all dead stems at their base. Plants are equally healthy and vigorous afterwards, provided they are fed and well tended.

Pruning: treat like shrub roses, but also cut out any vigorous upright stems that disturb the low profile of the plant.

■ **Miniature roses** are no more than about 45cm (18in) high, usually bushy, sometimes with a slightly tender constitution. **Pruning:** prune lightly to maintain size or fairly hard for improved flower quality, cutting all stems back to four or five buds.

■ **Standard roses** These are hybrid tea or floribunda roses grafted on a tall stem. **Pruning:** they should be pruned according to their type. Weeping standards are mostly grafted forms of rambler roses and are pruned in the same way as ramblers.

■ **Climbers and ramblers** Climbers have stiff stems and bear large flowers in flushes or throughout summer. Ramblers have long, flexible stems with smaller flowers in large trusses, usually borne in one display. **Pruning:** ramblers are pruned in summer (see page 75) and climbers are pruned in late winter (see page 136).

The three degrees of pruning

The basic pruning routine can be adapted for all kinds of rose. The severity of your pruning will affect the size, vigour and flowering of a rose. It needs to be adjusted according to the type and variety, and also the amount of growth it makes in your soil.

■ **Light pruning** Shorten older stems by no more than a third and remove the tips from young shoots. This restrains vigorous varieties, which would produce even stronger stems if they were hard pruned. It also maintains the size of the rose, especially on poor or dry soils.

■ **Moderate pruning** Cut the main stems to half their original length, and shorten weaker shoots to just two or three buds. This suits general garden purposes, ensuring a healthy balance between flowers and new growth.

■ **Hard pruning** Reduce the main stems to a height of two or three buds from the base. This technique is used for most shrub roses immediately after planting, but is otherwise reserved for hybrid teas intended for exhibition and for rejuvenating overgrown shrub roses.

Old, woody rose stems can become too tough and thick for secateurs to cut through. If this is the case, use a pruning saw or long-handled pruners to cut them back.

Giving shrub roses a moderate pruning

1 Dead stems should all be cut out and any parts that are damaged or diseased trimmed back to healthy wood. This will show a white surface when it is cut.

2 Thin, spindly shoots and suckers should be removed as well as any that cross one another or are growing into the centre of the plant.

3 The remaining strong, healthy branches should be shortened by half to an outward-facing bud or shoot. The prunings should be disposed of or composted.

4 To stimulate new growth, prune out one or two of the oldest branches to ground level using long-handled pruners.

Correct pruning keeps the plants to the desired size and shape, encouraging strong growth and plenty of flowers. Early spring is the time to put in new plants, particularly evergreens, and sow some annual climbers to enjoy their colourful, if short-lived, contribution to summer.

Spring checklist

■ **Plant new climbers** before the weather becomes warm and dry. Spring is the best time to plant evergreen climbers and wall shrubs, and any plants on the borderline of hardiness (see page 140).

■ **Prune winter jasmine** (*Jasminum nudiflorum*) if you have not already done so (see page 138), as well as overgrown deciduous climbers like common jasmine (*Jasminum officinale*) and honeysuckle.

■ **Prune clematis** that flower in summer and autumn (see page 32).

■ **Repair or replace supports** before climbers grow strongly. Tie new shoots to wires on fences or walls.

■ **Remove winter frost protection** as soon as weather conditions permit, but protect blooms of early flowering climbers such as *Akebia quinata* and *Clematis* 'Early Sensation' if late frosts are threatened. Cover with fleece overnight, but remove it during the day.

■ **Mulch all climbers** and apply a slow-release fertiliser.

■ **Sow annual climbers** in pots or trays and start off under cover (see right).

■ **Trim back self-clinging climbers,** such as ivy, to keep it away from woodwork, roofs and guttering.

■ **Pot up semi-ripe cuttings** taken in late summer, if rooted.

■ **Top-dress, feed and water** container-grown climbers.

■ **Prune out frost-damaged shoots** in April, cutting them back to healthy growth.

■ **Prune early flowering climbers** such as *Clematis alpina*, *C. macropetala* and *C. armandii*.

■ **Train the growing stems** of climbers into their supports.

Sowing seeds of morning glory

1 Using a six-cell tray, sow two or three seeds to a cell. The tray should then be stood in a warm place or put in a propagator.

2 As soon as seedlings appear after a week or so, move the tray to a well-lit spot. As they get bigger, transplant individual plants to 8cm (3in) pots and stake them as growth develops.

Sowing annual climbers

Annual climbers are splendid for summer colour. They grow rapidly from seed and may reach 2.5m (8ft) by the end of the season, and should be smothered in colourful blooms.

You can direct sow hardy annuals outside, but the best results come from seeds sown in pots or modular trays of moist potting compost. Half-hardy annuals must be raised under cover and planted out once frosts are past.

Sweet peas (see opposite) do best when protected in paper tubes or root trainers to develop their deep root system. Transfer hardy annuals to a cool, frost-free coldframe or greenhouse; half-hardy annuals need a warmer environment.

Herbaceous climbers

Herbaceous climbers like the golden hop (*Humulus lupulus* 'Aureus') and perennial peas, such as *Lathyrus rotundifolius*, die back over winter and leave dead stems. Get rid of dead stems now, before new shoots grow into them. Ideally, they should be cut back to ground level in late winter but with young plants it can be helpful to leave the first year's growth to support new stems.

Plant herbaceous climbers now to boost vertical displays later in the year. Secure supports and regular attention will reward you with a beautiful house wall or boundary.

Planting climbers

Before planting, improve the soil by digging in compost or other well-rotted organic matter together with a little bone meal or balanced fertiliser. If you are planting into a specially prepared hole in a paved area, fork the sides and base to make sure there is plenty of space for the roots to run, and that it drains freely.

An hour or two before you plant, water the climber thoroughly. Site your planting hole at least 45cm (18in) from the wall; if there is an overhanging roof or gutter, move it farther out. Plant climbers slightly deeper than the level of compost in the container. With clematis, plant more deeply so that 8–10cm (3–4in) of the stems are covered. If the top growth is spindly and thin, cut it back hard to a bud at soil level.

After planting, continue to water at regular intervals until established but do not feed until next year. Keep their base and roots shaded with a thick mulch, paving slabs or low-growing plants.

Methods of support

Almost all climbers need to be trained and most need to be tied to a support, which should be positioned before planting. Even those that cling by stem rootlets or sucker pads, such as ivy, climbing hydrangea (*H. anomala* ssp. *petiolaris*) or virginia creeper

Planting out sweet peas

1 Position canes 2.5m (8ft) long 30–45cm (12–18in) apart in rows or as wigwams. Make sure they are firm.
2 Plant one potful or paper tube of sweet peas next to each cane using a trowel or dibber; water in well.
3 Using a loop of string or special sweet pea rings secure young shoots to the cane. Once the plants start growing, tie in new growth every two or three days.

(*Parthenocissus*), will need your help.

■ **Horizontal training wires** are the simplest and most effective system. Stretch them taut along the wall or between fence posts, anchoring them at 2m (6ft) intervals with 'vine eyes' (special nails or screws with a hole at one end). Space wires roughly 45cm (18in) apart, with the bottom one this distance above the ground. Use stout galvanised wire, and make sure the anchor points are strong enough to bear the weight of a large climber.

■ **Trellis is an attractive** alternative to wires. Make sure panels are held clear of the wall or fence so that air can pass between plant and structure, and to make tying in easier. Mount panels on wooden battens and secure with long strong screws.

Planting a climber

The hole you dig should be larger and deeper than is needed for the rootball. Once dug, tip in bone meal and compost. Turn the climber out of its pot and tease out congested roots. Place the rootball in the hole, planting fractionally deeper than the level of compost in the container. Backfill with soil, firming it down gently with your foot. Water thoroughly. Tie stems to a support.

■ **Tie stems loosely to the wires or trellis,** using soft garden string. Plants that cling by tendrils, such as clematis, or twine, like honeysuckle (*Lonicera*), need little more than to have wayward stems secured. Non-clinging plants such as roses and wall shrubs need their stems tied at several points while they are young and flexible.

Training climbers

Flowering climbers especially should be trained in a fan formation, gently angling the main stems away from the vertical. This promotes flowering and ensures the wall or fence is evenly covered all the way down to the ground, rather than merely at the top.

Keep wall shrubs, roses and other climbers that need regular pruning on the outside of the trellis or wires. If the stems extend between support and wall, they are difficult to unravel and will become jammed, sometimes forcing the trellis or vine eyes away from the wall.

Pruning climbers

With the majority of climbers (honeysuckles, jasmines, early flowering clematis, for example), pruning is only necessary to repair winter damage or restore plants to the desired shape. The basic rules are simple: if the climber flowers in spring, prune straight after flowering; if it flowers in summer or autumn, prune in late winter or early spring. Remove any dead or damaged branches, and carefully tease out and dispose of old and weak stems. Tie in loose stems, bending them away from the vertical.

Pruning clematis

The severity of pruning will vary according to the flowering time of the variety. However, clematis are seldom harmed whether left untouched or pruned almost to ground level.

■ **Large-flowered clematis** that bloom in early to midsummer, such as 'Lasurstern', 'Nelly Moser' and 'The President': first, remove all dead, damaged or weak shoots, then cut back healthy stems to a strong pair of buds. Hard prune some shoots and lightly prune others for a plant that flowers from top to bottom.

■ **Species and large-flowered hybrids** that bloom in late summer, such as 'Ernest Markham', 'Gipsy Queen', 'Jackmanii', *Clematis tangutica* and *C. viticella* and its hybrids: cut back all stems to 30–60cm (1–2ft), just above a strong pair of buds.

■ **Summer and autumn-flowering clematis** are pruned in winter or early spring.

■ **Early flowering species,** including *Clematis alpina*, may need pruning in late spring (this can be left until early summer). Although they perform well without any pruning, if you need to tidy them or restrict their size, the best time to act is as soon as the flowers are over. Trimming back encourages the plant to make strong growth on which flower buds will form next year. *C. montana*, which flowers in spring, is more usually pruned in early summer.

Pruning evergreen clematis

Unlike most early flowering clematis, the vigorous evergreen *Clematis armandii* benefits from drastic treatment, particularly if it has been neglected or is growing in a restricted space.

■ **Wait until flowers have faded** then cut off all the growth, right back to the trunk.
■ **If the plant is healthy,** it will sprout in a couple of weeks. The young stems will be vigorous but brittle. Tie them in carefully as they emerge, using soft garden string and gently bending them to a horizontal position.
■ **Continue to train the stems,** arranging them so that they cover as much of the wall or fence as possible. Stems on a mature plant should grow to about 3m (10ft) by late summer, and will produce a superb display of fragrant white flowers in early spring.

Propagating clematis

Spring is the season to propagate late-flowering *Clematis viticella* and its hybrids. This can be done by taking cuttings or by layering.

Cuttings To take leaf-bud cuttings (see below), select healthy young stems that are beginning to turn woody. Roots will form at the leaf buds, which will start to grow in five to ten weeks.

Layering This is the easiest method of propagating mature clematis (see also page 140) and now is a good time to begin.
■ **Take a low-growing stem.** On the underside, make a small slanting cut without severing the stem – or simply scrape off the bark.
■ **Anchor the wounded part** in the ground, just below the surface, using a stone or wire staple.
■ **Within a year,** the plant will have grown roots and, as soon as it is dormant, it can be transplanted to its site in the garden.

Taking leaf-bud cuttings of clematis

1 To take a cutting, remove a whole stem from the plant. Trim the base and discard the soft, fleshy top, cutting just above a pair of leaf buds. You should be left with a stem that is about 5cm (2in) long.

2 Fill a tray or shallow pot that has plenty of drainage holes with a mixture of equal parts perlite or fine grit and soil-less potting compost. Insert each cutting so that the leaf buds at the top are in contact with the compost.

3 Place the tray or pot in a propagator or on a windowsill. Inspect the cuttings regularly and remove any that are turning black or rotting immediately. Once they are rooted, they can be potted up.

As early flowering shrubs and trees produce abundant blossom, it is time to trim evergreens into shape and focus on pruning and propagation. Restore overgrown hedges and plant new evergreens and specimen shrubs, before returning to early varieties to prune them back into shape after flowering.

Spring checklist

■ **Continue planting deciduous species,** but try to get all bare-rooted plants in the ground by the end of March.

■ **Refirm recent plantings** if their roots have been lifted by wind or frost. If dry, water and mulch to keep the roots moist.

■ **Inspect supports and tree ties,** and repair or adjust where necessary.

■ **Cover vulnerable plants** such as cistus and hydrangeas if frost threatens, and shelter recently planted evergreens.

■ **Take prompt action** to prevent pests and diseases spreading; some evergreen diseases, such as mahonia rust, are present or visible all the year round (see page 37).

■ **Prune late-flowering shrubs** such as buddleia, perovskia and caryopteris, and frost-shy shrubs like hydrangeas and hardy fuchsias (see pages 37–8).

■ **Trim winter-flowering heaths** and heathers to remove dead blooms and keep plants compact.

■ **Start pruning early flowering shrubs** such as forsythia and winter jasmine (see page 37) as their display finishes.

■ **Prune mahonias** to prevent leggy growth (see page 37).

■ **Hard prune shrubs with coloured stems,** such as cornus and salix, to encourage vivid young growth, and cut back canes of white-stemmed brambles (*Rubus*) to the ground.

■ **Prune overgrown evergreen** shrubs and hedges to renovate them in late March.

■ **Move misplaced** evergreen shrubs growing on heavy soil.

Forsythias, hardy and easily grown, produce a profusion of vibrant yellow flowers, making them one of the glories of a spring garden.

■ **Pull up or cut off suckers** from shrubs such as lilac and sumach, or mow them off if they are growing in a lawn (see page 146).

■ **Layer shrubs and trees** that are difficult to propagate from cuttings. Plants with low pliable branches can be layered in the ground, while those with stiffer upright stems are better air layered.

■ **Sow tree and shrub seeds** that have been stored over winter.

■ **Pot up seedlings and cuttings** started last autumn, and grow on ready for planting in a nursery bed in early summer.

■ **Trim rose hedges in late March** and prune out any dead and diseased wood. Feed after pruning.

■ **Water plants in containers** if droughts or winds have dried out the compost.

■ **Prune shrubs** that have flowered already, and hard prune shrubs that flower later on new shoots (see page 36).

■ **Water shrubs and trees** planted in early spring regularly, especially on light soils.

■ **Feed young trees and shrubs,** and any you have pruned hard, with a balanced fertiliser; water in if the soil is at all dry.

■ **Restore overgrown deciduous hedges** (see page 117) before birds start nesting.

■ **Continue protecting foliage** and flower buds at risk from frost (including many silver and grey shrubs, such as cistus, halimium and romneya), with fleece.

■ **Check for dead and frost-damaged** shoots once the risk of frost has passed; prune them back to uninjured wood.

■ **Tidy and weed** around established trees and shrubs, but don't damage surface roots.

■ **Pull up weeds** by hand around those trees and shrubs, such as magnolias, that dislike root disturbance. Alternatively, deter weeds with a heavy mulch.

■ **Watch out for pests and diseases,** especially aphids and caterpillars, and mildew in a dry season.

■ **Mulch warmed soil** during May to conserve moisture around younger plants, those recently planted and any on light soils.

■ **Deadhead rhododendrons and azaleas** that have finished flowering.

■ **Plant new evergreens** as the soil starts to warm up (see page 36).

■ **Put up temporary windbreaks** around newly planted evergreens.

■ **Take soft-tip cuttings** of shrubs and hedge plants that produce long new growths (see page 39).

■ **Prune the stems of** *Buddleja davidii* to varying heights, to produce an attractive, tiered display of flowers. Spread the pruning over several weeks, which will extend the flowering season.

■ **Plant bamboos,** both as specimen shrubs and for decorative windbreaks. Where space is limited, choose clump-forming species rather than spreading varieties with potentially invasive runners.

Avoiding the dangers of late frost

Use fleece or similar temporary cover to protect vulnerable plants when frost threatens. Spring frosts are unpredictable and can be lethal to flower buds, young growth and plants that originated in warm climates. These include camellias (below), grey and silver-leaved shrubs, hydrangeas and some magnolias.

Planting new evergreens

Evergreen trees and shrubs can be planted safely during mid and late spring as the soil warms up and conditions improve. This is often preferable in cold regions and on heavy wet soils, where autumn planting can result in root injury or disease. Plants that are root-balled or bare-rooted should be planted by the beginning of April; container-grown specimens are also best established now before a hot and dry summer season.

Trees and shrubs have a potentially long life in one place, so the planting site needs thorough preparation. Dig the soil down two spade depths, and improve the drainage where necessary. Remove all weeds and weed root fragments from a wide area around the planting site. For a tree, drive in a short, upright support stake, slightly off-centre, before planting.

If planting a container-grown evergreen, water the new plant in its pot and allow to drain. Then remove the pot and tease some of the roots away from the rootball. Put root-balled plants in position, then cut and remove the netting around the roots. Back-fill the hole with excavated soil and firm the plant in place with your foot. Water well and cover the area with a thick mulch.

Secure a tree to its stake with one or two adjustable tree ties. On exposed sites, it is a good idea to erect a screen of fine mesh or similar windbreak material while the plant is getting established. Place it on the windward side of the plant to shield it from frost and cold winds.

Pruning shrubs

There is a lot of pruning to do at this time of year. Some of it is cosmetic, but for many species pruning is an essential stimulus to prolific flowering later on.

Pruning evergreens Laurel, holly and rhododendrons are typical of evergreen shrubs that require little annual pruning – just shorten last year's new shoots by half.

Hard pruning a box hedge

1 Using marker posts and string, set the line at the desired height and cut the top of the hedge using hedging shears.
2 Trim branches back almost to the main stems once you have cleared away clippings from the top of the hedge.

If they become straggly or outgrow their space you can hard prune – cut them back radically between late March and early June to stumps about 45–60cm (18–24in) high. Remove damaged or diseased wood and weak growth, leaving the strongest stumps to regrow. Overgrown evergreen hedges, like box, holly and yew, are treated similarly (see above), but the work is better spread over a few years to ensure even regrowth.

■ **Cut the top** to the required height, then trim all the branches on one side almost back to the main stems. Feed and mulch the hedge; water well in dry weather.
■ **When new shoots are growing** well on the cut face, which may be two or three years later, the second side may be hard pruned in the same way.

Winter and early flowering shrubs

This is pruning time for shrubs that bloomed late last year and those that have just finished flowering. Shrubs such as winter-flowering *Viburnum* x *bodnantense* and

V. x *burkwoodii*, which flowers early on stems produced the previous year, are pruned as soon as blooms fade. New stems grow freely from the base, so cut out about a third of the oldest branches and trim the rest to shape; in this way, plants are rejuvenated with enhanced flowering.

Late-flowering shrubs

Most late-flowering shrubs, including *Buddleja davidii*, caryopteris, lavatera, leycesteria, perovskia and santolina, produce their blooms on growth made in the current year. These stems need pruning now, just before or as their new leaves begin to open.

■ **Shorten shoots** that flowered last year to within one or two buds from their base.
■ **Thin congested** growth by removing or shortening some of the older stems.

Regenerating shrubs

If neglected or only lightly pruned over a number of years, shrubs such as cornus, *Buddleja davidii* and many hydrangeas become tall and leggy, with a bare base and fewer, small flowers. You can often rejuvenate them by cutting them hard back in early spring, leaving a series of healthy stumps to regrow. Small shrubs can be cut back in one go but larger specimens, such as mature hydrangeas, are better tackled in stages, spreading the work over two or three years. Feed after pruning and leave the new growth unpruned for a year to become established. Always check when you buy a shrub that it withstands hard pruning because some kinds, such as broom (*Cytisus*), do not regenerate well.

Pruning mahonias

Tall mahonias such as *Mahonia japonica* develop long bare stems unless pruned annually. You can prune shorter-growing *M. aquifolium* in the same way, unless it is grown as a hedge or ground cover, in which case shear off all the stems, almost to ground level, to keep growth young and leafy. You can use the prunings to propagate (see page 84).

■ **Mahonia rust** is present all year round and causes deep reddish purple patches on older leaves, with powdery brown pustules on the undersides. Prune and burn diseased foliage, and spray young growth with copper-based fungicide at monthly intervals during the growing season.

Pruning hydrangeas

This is the best time to prune hydrangeas such as *Hydrangea paniculata*, *H. arborescens* and *H. macrophylla* hybrids – both lacecap and mophead (hortensia) types. The dead flowers are usually left untouched over winter, because they are considered to provide a degree of frost protection.

■ **Cut old flowering stems** to two or three buds from the base.
■ **Remove any weak** or exhausted shoots.
■ **Mulch** with a deep layer of rotted manure.

Pruning hardy fuchsias

Fuchsias are often left until spring before pruning, especially in colder gardens, as old growth provides frost protection. Now all this must be cut back hard, almost to ground level. In milder areas you can prune more lightly, allowing a framework of permanent older

Late March to early June is the time to renovate an overgrown laurel hedge, which will ensure plenty of healthy new growth.

branches to develop. Then remove any framework branches that are exhausted, shorten the sideshoots to their base and lightly trim the remaining stems to shape.

Pruning cotinus
Prune smokebush (*Cotinus*) now, according to the effect you require. Cutting back large bushes hard will restore their shape and vigour, stimulating more handsome and colourful foliage, whereas light pruning maintains size and allows the bush to flower more lavishly.

Hedge care
A hedge acts as a natural boundary, which will constantly rejuvenate if well cared for. It can also act as the perfect backdrop for more colourful garden plants.

- **Tidy leaves and dead wood** from the base of hedges, and clear weeds. Watch out especially for perennial and twining weeds that can soon infiltrate dense hedges.
- **Water newly planted hedges** regularly in dry weather. Concentrate water at the base of each plant rather than giving the hedge an overall sprinkling. Check every two weeks unless rain intervenes.

- **Feed young hedges** with a balanced fertiliser at a rate of 125g per sq m (4oz per sq yd), distributed evenly around the plants. Older hedges need only half this rate, unless they have been hard pruned to shape. A mulch of rotted manure or garden compost can replace the spring feed on established hedges.
- **Mulch young hedges** liberally with grass mowings in dry weather and on light soils. Spread a mulch 5cm (2in) deep over moist soil and keep the level topped up as the season progresses.
- **You can give formal conifer** and other fast-growing hedges, such as privet and *Lonicera nitida*, their first clip of the year now, using shears or a hedge trimmer (see page 87). As an aid to trimming, stretch a taut line between two canes and use this guide to ensure accurate cutting and to define the new height.

TIP Where a hedge acts as a windbreak, you can sculpt the top in free-form undulations or castellate it like battlements. This helps to filter the wind, whereas a level top makes the hedge behave more like a solid wall or fence, causing wind turbulence.

Trimming a privet hedge

1 Working from the bottom of the hedge up, begin by clipping the sides of the privet. Brush off loose trimmings as you go so you can see the shape properly.

2 It is traditional to trim the sides to a slight batter (an inward lean), so that light can reach the base of the hedge. However, an upright profile can also be used.

3 Using a stake and string, clip the top to the line. To ensure a consistent level, trim a wide hedge in two stages, working to the middle from each side.

Propagation

You can increase your stock of shrubs and hedge plants using the simple procedures of layering and taking softwood cuttings, which are best done now.

Layering bushy shrubs The lower branches of many shrubs naturally develop roots where they touch the ground. You can exploit this ability to produce new plants with little risk of failure, because the new plant remains attached to its parent until rooted. You may do this at any time of year, although starting now, when growth is at its most vigorous, allows a full season's growth before the new shrub is severed and transplanted in autumn.

■ **For bushy shrubs** such as rosemary, ornamental quince, cistus, virburnums and rhododendrons, select a healthy, flexible, low shoot that will bend easily to touch the ground 15–20cm (6–8in) near its tip.

■ **Where it touches** the ground, scoop out some of the soil with a trowel to leave a shallow depression.

■ **Strip the leaves** from the shoot at the point of contact, and wound the underside to expose some of the inner tissues. This can be done by slicing off a thin layer of bark with a sharp knife, by cutting a small slit at an angle to about halfway through or simply by twisting the stem.

■ **Peg the stem down** and cover the rooting area with soil.

■ **Should rooting not occur,** carefully reopen the wound, dust the surfaces with hormone powder and try again. Wait until spring or the following autumn before detaching the shoot from the parent plant and moving it to its new home.

Taking soft-tip cuttings In mid to late spring, many shrubs produce long new shoots that are firm enough for you to take cuttings. Hebe, lavatera, sage, phlomis and santolina are a few of the many species easily and quickly propagated like this.

Soft-tip cuttings

Soft-tip cuttings are a good way to propagate certain shrubs. Trim a small piece of healthy stem just below a leaf joint and remove the bottom pair of leaves. Insert the cuttings into pots or modular trays of sharp sand and leave them in a mini-propagator or on a windowsill out of direct sunlight until they take root.

■ **Trim each shoot** to about 5–8cm (2–3in) long, cutting just below a leaf joint.

■ **Remove leaves from the lower half** of the cutting and pinch out its soft tip, which can sometimes rot and encourage disease. If the base of the cutting is firm or starting to look woody, dip it in hormone powder or liquid to help stimulate rooting.

■ **Insert the cuttings** to just below the lowest leaves in a pot or tray of cuttings compost or a 50:50 mixture of potting compost and grit or sharp sand. Make sure the cuttings are well spaced out and do not touch each other.

■ **Water in well** and leave to drain. Stand the pot in a closed propagator or cover it with a clear plastic bag (keep it off the leaves by supporting it with wire hoops). Keep warm and lightly shaded from bright sunshine. New, paler top growth and roots appearing from the base of the pot indicate that rooting has been successful.

Start planning and planting pots now, so you can enjoy a colourful patio display right through the summer. Seasonal and permanent plants grown in containers and raised beds rely entirely on you for their care, so begin a feeding and watering routine from late spring for the best results.

Spring checklist

■ **Clean patios and decking** before the space is filled with container displays.

■ **Remove winter protection** and return pots to their original positions as soon as the weather permits. However, keep some fleece handy to protect susceptible young growth and flowers if late frosts threaten.

■ **Brighten up your containers** and patio borders with spring bedding plants that are tough, colourful and long flowering. There is plenty of choice in garden centres or nurseries, including double daisies (*Bellis perennis*), forget-me-nots, primulas and wallflowers, plus ready-grown bulbs.

■ **Water regularly** as the weather warms up, particularly on breezy days when containers dry out rapidly.

■ **Order young, tender perennials** and bedding plants from a mail-order catalogue or internet supplier.

■ **Protect the blooms** of spring-flowering shrubs like camellias, rhododendrons and azaleas by placing containers in a sheltered spot away from the early morning sun.

■ **Mulch rhododendrons** with chipped bark to protect their shallow roots from extremes of temperature.

■ **Feed spring bulbs** in containers until the leaves start to yellow and die, so they will make a good display next spring. Label each container so you can identify dormant bulbs.

■ **Deadhead winter pansies** to encourage new flowers.

■ **Plant lily bulbs** to twice their depth in soil-based potting compost. Put three bulbs in a 25–30cm (10–12in) deep pot and stand in an unheated greenhouse, coldframe or a sheltered spot outside.

■ **Plant up containers** of tender plants in a heated greenhouse or conservatory.

Pansies are short-lived evergreen perennials that are ideal for containers. Deadheading them will prolong their flowering display.

Small plug plants, available from garden centres and mail-order companies (see opposite), are useful for hanging baskets (see page 45) and flower pouches. By growing the displays under cover through spring, you will have well-established containers to put out after the frosts.

■ **Plant perennials,** ornamental grasses and ferns in pots. Many of them make ideal low-maintenance container plants and they will establish quickly if planted up now. Good-looking foliage and early flowering perennials are particularly useful during spring when there is little else around in the garden. Some tolerate shade and so are perfect for brightening gloomy corners. Move them into bare patches in beds.

■ **Prune patio roses,** removing all dead, weak and damaged shoots and shortening the sideshoots.

■ **Top-dress permanent plants** by replacing the top few centimetres of compost with an appropriate compost mixed with a suitable fertiliser (see pages 42–3).

■ **Pot up roses** and shrubs (see page 45) as permanent container plants.

■ **Harden off shrubs** of borderline hardiness that overwintered under cover (see page 148) in April, so that they acclimatise to outside conditions before being returned to the patio in late spring.

■ **Control weeds** in paving cracks at an early stage by hand, with a weedkiller or garden flame gun. If you like an informal garden, once the cracks are clear, sow seed of plants that thrive in crevices such as mexican daisy (*Erigeron karvinskianus*) and yellow fumitory (*Corydalis lutea*).

■ **Bring garden furniture out of store.** Resin furniture only requires washing with hot water and a mild detergent. Wooden furniture usually needs treating with stain or preservative every other year.

■ **Plant out half-hardy bedding plants** as soon as the risk of frost has passed, usually late May. You will still find plenty of summer bedding plants in garden centres and other outlets, even though it is too late to order plants by mail or over the internet.

■ **Prepare the soil** in raised beds and patio borders ready for planting by removing any weeds and forking in plenty of organic matter, such as rotted manure or mushroom compost. Apply a general fertiliser before planting up.

■ **Plant annual climbers** in containers or raised beds to bring an extra colourful dimension to the patio. Nasturtiums and sweet peas look charming growing up a wigwam of bamboo canes or rustic poles.

■ **Plant some herbs,** not only for kitchen use but for their fragrance. Plant them by hot paving – the heat will help to release their aromatic oils. Lavenders, rosemary,

Plug plants

1 You can buy young plants for containers by mail-order or via the internet. Many varieties are sold as plug plants, which will arrive in their own packaging

2 Plug plants should be potted on into 8cm (3in) pots straight away. Allow them to grow to a reasonable size before transplanting into your chosen containers.

sage, marjoram, coriander and basil all grow in hot, dry conditions.

■ **Start to think** about containers and hanging baskets for a summer patio display (see page 44). Achieve dramatic results by restricting yourself to simple colour schemes, using foliage as well as flowers.

■ **Plant up pots or raised beds** with summer bedding to provide a colourful splash from July onwards. Or choose unusual flowering perennial plants, like *Agastache*, and bulbs such as the glorious South African pineapple lily (*Eucomis*).

■ **Direct sow hardy annuals** in pots or raised beds (see page 19).

■ **Introduce tender shrubs** in large containers. A lemon or pomegranate plant, for example, will provide a wonderful summer display, but must be taken indoors in late autumn.

Cleaning patios and decking

Patios, decks and paths look much better for a thorough cleaning at the end of winter. They are also safer to walk on as algae can make surfaces dangerously slippery. Shady areas are the worst affected by moss and algae, as the surface tends to stay damp for long periods. The best method of cleaning is to use a pressure washer, but first make sure that the water can drain away freely.

You can use the washer alone or in conjunction with an environmentally friendly proprietary cleaner. Apply cleaner before using the washer and carefully follow the manufacturer's instructions. Bear in mind the following points:

■ **Paviours and some types of slab** may be damaged if water is applied at high pressure. On these surfaces, use moderate pressure of around 1000 psi, or hold the applicator high above the surface of the paving to lessen the force of the water.

■ **When cleaning concrete** do not focus pressure on a single area for more than a few seconds – it could damage the surface.

■ **Patios should slope gently** to allow water to drain readily, so start at the highest point and work downhill.

A pressure washer will remove dangerously slippery algae, but make sure it does not wash the mortar out from between slabs.

■ **For decking,** use low pressure of around 750 psi. Water applied at high pressure can drive dirt into the wood. After cleaning, allow decking to dry, then apply a sealer to the surface.

Care of container shrubs

Most evergreens are at their peak of growth in spring and should not be trimmed or pruned until summer.

■ **Dwarf rhododendrons and camellias** should have their old flowers and seed heads removed.

■ **Early flowering deciduous shrubs** generally benefit from being pruned as soon as flowering is over; remove branches that have flowered to encourage leafy growth in summer and even more flowers next year (see page 36).

■ **Few topiary specimens** need clipping in late spring, apart from plants that grow rapidly and need several clips a year. Trim privet (*Ligustrum*) and *Lonicera nitida* now, following the original shape. Use small shears, or even scissors, to keep to the precise outline.

■ **Give roses a light feed** in late spring and treat to prevent mildew, black spot and aphid attack.

Feeding

Patio plants get hungry, especially during summer. The more permanent shrubs and trees planted in open ground will need little by way of plant food by now, since their roots will be searching for nutrients over a wide area. But plants grown in containers, raised beds or borders – where soil is in any way limited – will need feeding regularly from late spring onwards.

■ **Liquid feeds** can be given every seven to 14 days when watering the plants, throughout the growing season. Start six weeks after planting, when the fertiliser in the compost will have run out. Use a high-potash feed, such as tomato fertiliser, to promote flowers.

■ **Slow-release fertilisers** provide all the necessary nutrients container plants require for several months, or even the whole growing season – check the manufacturer's instructions. They release more nutrients as temperatures rise and the moisture available increases – just when the plants need them most.

TIP Avoid over-feeding container-grown plants. It makes their growth too lush and they can become prone to diseases and disorders. The results of over-feeding are more of a problem than plant starvation, especially in pot-grown plants on patios. Remember that plants manufacture the bulk of their own food from sunlight, water and carbon dioxide in the air; substances absorbed through the roots are merely supplements – essential, but needed only in the smallest quantities.

Watering

Watering is the most important task in container gardening. More plants suffer stress through lack of water than from any other cause.

■ **Water new plants** thoroughly, not only when planted but regularly until their root systems have developed.

■ **Water plants in containers** and hanging baskets daily as summer approaches. An automatic watering system is ideal for this.

■ **Check small patio beds** with shallow soil as they dry out fast. Even after rain it is worth checking just below the surface in case the soil is bone dry. A thorough soaking every two weeks in warm, dry weather makes all the difference to the way your patio plants perform.

Tulips, planted in autumn, make a striking and rewarding display in spring, especially when planted in groups in a pot.

Creating a summer display

Well-planted pots and hanging baskets will cheer up the patio in summer. Use colourful bedding and plant generously to stage as bright a display as possible.

Summer containers Garden centres have a wide range of bedding and other plants for summer containers. They are often presented in colour groups, so it is easy to choose those that fit a colour scheme. The many flower shows and plant fairs that take place at this time of year also offer a range of interesting plants.

■ **'Anchor' plants** are central to a container, whether used alone or surrounded by smaller or trailing plants. Fuchsias are a popular choice, but *Solanum rantonnetii* trained as a standard or succulents like *Aeonium arboreum* and the century plant (*Agave americana*) also make fine 'anchors'.

■ **Trailing or filling plants** to go with the 'anchors' include yellow bidens and blue scaevola. New varieties of pelargonium are bred every year, but many older kinds, especially those with aromatic leaves, are just as beautiful and easy to grow.

■ **Use fragrance** as well as colour. Heliotrope has a bewitching scent, as do mignonettes, tobacco plants, night-scented stocks and sweet peas.

■ **Newly purchased plants** for bedding and containers need to be exposed gradually to cold, windy or excessively wet weather before they go outside. This is known as 'hardening off' (see page 15).

■ **Water containers daily** from late spring onwards and feed every 7–14 days during the growing season, from six weeks after planting. Use a high-potash feed, such as tomato fertiliser.

Hanging baskets The most attractive baskets are those with plants growing through the sides as well as out of the top. When planting, aim for an almost perfect sphere of foliage and flower.

■ **Line baskets** with moss or a lining made from coconut-fibre or recycled cardboard. Black plastic is practical but less attractive.

Planting a summer container

1 A patio pot needs to be large, at least 40cm (16in) across the top and with a drainage hole. Fill it two-thirds full with soil-less potting compost.
2 Position the plants, placing the 'anchor' in the centre. When satisfied, remove them and make a hole large enough for the anchor plant's rootball.
3 Place filling and trailing plants around the 'anchor', encouraging the trailers to grow over the sides. Add more compost between the plants, firm them into position and water thoroughly.

■ **After planting** a hanging basket, wash off any compost that has lodged on the leaves, preferably using rainwater. The plants will take a few days to orientate themselves and will then begin to fill the space.

■ **Suspend a hanging basket** from a strong hook well secured to a wall or strong support. It should be in full light and sheltered from wind. Make sure the basket is easy to reach for watering and that it will not be in your way.

■ **For a good display,** hanging baskets require regular feeding and constant watering; in hot weather they may need watering at least twice a day. Mix water-retaining gel into the soil-less compost to reduce the rate at which moisture is lost.

Selecting permanent plants

Small shrubs and trees help to give an outdoor seating area more character. Evergreens will provide interest all year round and brighten the garden scene in winter. Select the permanent plants in a mixed container first to create a framework.

Trees and shrubs Choose varieties that are fairly small or slow growing as rooting space is limited. Japanese maples are ideal small trees because they grow at a gentle pace and, provided they have a sheltered, partially shaded spot, are shapely and statuesque. Their autumn colour, winter outline and spring foliage make them great year-rounders, and they grow well in a roomy container.

Patio roses Roses are popular for containers on terraces and patios, but it is important to select those that suit hot, sunny patio conditions.

■ **Choose disease-resistant varieties** that are bred to ensure good health in normal garden conditions.

■ **Check they will flower all summer.** True patio roses, such as the pink, fragrant *Rosa* Queen Mother, yellow *R.* Perestroika or *R.*

Planting a hanging basket

1 The first step is to select a liner for your wire mesh basket. Either use a thick layer of natural moss, black plastic or one of the alternative liners available. Fill to about a third with soil-less potting compost. Then balance the basket on a bucket or a big pot so that you can work with both hands.

2 Position the plants in the basket, gently teasing the roots through the mesh sides and the liner. Firm them into the compost by hand. Add more compost and insert more moss and plants as you go, working in layers.

3 Once the sides are completed, plant the top of the basket, then firm the plants and water thoroughly.

Scarlet Patio, keep flowering as long as you deadhead throughout summer.

■ **Try to choose** varieties for fragrance.

Patio climbers Climbing plants can be grown in containers. Vigorous grape vines or wisteria trained on frames or pergolas create a shady canopy in summer but let in more sunshine when their leaves fall in autumn. Climbing roses – including small, bright coppery-hued *R.* Warm Welcome – can be used in this way or trained over arches around the patio's edge.

Now that the lawn is starting to grow again, it is time to get it into good condition for the year ahead. Attention now will influence the appearance of your lawn throughout the summer. Give it a regular spring clean to clear moss, weeds and dead grass, and to encourage strong growth in the future.

Spring checklist

■ **Keep off the lawn** if it is frosted or the ground is sodden.

■ **Brush off any worm casts** when they appear on the surface of the lawn.

■ **Trim the edge** of your lawn by using a half-moon edging tool (see opposite) and repair any broken edges if necessary (see page 123).

■ **Level any humps or hollows** that have developed in the lawn over the winter months (see page 123).

An aerator introduces air into the soil and aerates grass roots before top dressing is applied in early spring. This also improves drainage and eases surface compaction.

■ **Aerate the lawn** with a hollow-tiner, spiked roller or garden fork; this improves drainage, eases surface compaction, and helps to get it back into condition for the season ahead.

■ **After aerating the lawn,** apply a top-dressing of equal parts loam, sand and peat substitute at a rate of 1.5kg per square metre (3lb per sq yd). For heavier soils with a high clay content, use a mix of four parts horticultural sand to one part loam or garden compost.

■ **Re-seed** any bare patches that have appeared (see opposite).

■ **Start feeding** with a spring fertiliser.

■ **Control any moss** that has built up in the lawn over winter (see page 49).

■ **Prepare the site** for a new lawn.
Thorough cultivation is essential for a good quality lawn, and problems created by taking short cuts are difficult to rectify later. Cultivate down to at least 30cm (12in), as the roots of many grasses can penetrate to this depth.

■ **Brush the lawn** to knock off any heavy dew. If it is left, the humid conditions can encourage the spread of fungal disease.

■ **Control isolated weeds** by spot treating with a liquid or gel weedkiller that is sprayed or brushed onto the leaves.

■ **Treat weed-infested lawns** with a combination method (see opposite).

■ **Scarify the lawn** to get rid of thatch (see page 49).

■ **Start mowing the lawn** when the grass begins to grow, which is once the soil temperature has risen to 5–7°C (40–45°F) (see page 48).

■ **Look out for yellow patches** on your lawn. This may be a sign of 'snow mould' or leatherjacket grubs.

Trimming a lawn edge

1 To give your lawn a clean, sharp edge, use a half-moon edging tool. On straight edges, stand on a plank and use this as a cutting guide.
2 Use long-handled edging shears to keep the lawn neat during the rest of the growing season.

Trimming lawn edges

The edge of a lawn often sags and crumbles as a result of frost action on the bare soil. Remove the narrowest strip possible to reinstate a clean edge; collect the trimmings and add them to the compost heap.

Dealing with bare patches

These may be due to weeds smothering the grass or part of the lawn having been covered and the grass dying due to lack of light. Sometimes, a spill of concentrated fertiliser or some other chemical can 'burn' the grass and kill it. Whatever the cause, these areas can be re-seeded to restore the lawn to its original condition (see right).

Weed control

In spring, the grass grows increasingly fast and so do the weeds. The best time to apply a combined chemical and cultural treatment is in late spring, when the grass is growing vigorously and will not be damaged by the weed-control measures.

Re-seeding bare patches

1 Rake vigorously with a spring-tined rake to remove all the old dead grass and to score the soil surface. To break up the surface and ease soil compaction, use a garden fork. Jab the tines into the soil to a depth of 2–3cm (1in).

2 Next, rake the soil to a depth of 1–2cm (½–¾in) to level it and to create seedbed with no lumps.

3 Sow the grass seed evenly over the area, at a rate of about 30g per square metre (1oz per square yard), then rake it in lightly.

4 The re-seeded area should then be covered with sacking, pinned down at the corners with canes, until seeds germinate; water in dry weather.

Apply a selective hormone weedkiller to the entire lawn. These weedkillers contain chemicals that cause the leaves and stems of weeds to twist, distort and grow upright. The weeds are weakened but are also within reach of the mower blades, making this a combination of chemical and cultural control. If weeds have been allowed to establish in a lawn, it may take several treatments to eradicate them, even to the extent of using different weedkillers on different occasions.

Use a purpose-made 'grubber' or an old kitchen knife to prise out weeds individually if you prefer not to use chemicals.

Mowing the lawn

Once the soil temperature rises above 5–7°C (40–45°F), the grass starts growing and you need to mow. The exact timing will vary from year to year, depending on the weather. Make the first cuts with the mower blades set high. As the rate of growth increases, the lawn will need more frequent mowing and the height of cut can gradually be lowered. Aim to reduce the grass by a third of its height at each cutting; do not cut it too short, as this weakens the grass and exposes bare soil where moss and weeds can easily establish.

Weedkiller safety

■ **Read and follow** the instructions exactly.
■ **Keep weedkillers locked away** from children and pets.
■ **Always wash your hands** after using any garden chemicals.
■ **Never mix weedkillers** with any other garden chemicals.
■ **Never decant weedkillers** into unmarked containers; it's important to clearly identify any potentially harmful chemicals.
■ **Never dispose** of any weedkiller down the drain; pour it onto a bare patch of soil away from plants. (Once in contact with soil the chemicals become inactive.)

In cold areas, late spring will be the earliest you start cutting your lawn; the heavier the soil, the longer it takes to warm up. In mild areas, where the soil never freezes, you may have mown several times by now. Wherever you are, always begin by giving the shaggy lawn a light trim, with the mower blades on the highest setting. The golden rule is never to reduce the length of the grass by more than a third at a single cut, as this will damage the lawn.

Feeding lawns

Regular mowing gradually saps the strength of the grass. If the nutrients taken up by the grass – that is then removed as clippings – are not replaced, the lawn will lose its vigour and become vulnerable to attack from disease. Overcome this problem by feeding the grass as soon as growth starts in the spring.

All spring lawn feeds contain high levels of nitrogen to promote rapid, green leaf growth. Most consist of a mixture of fertilisers designed to release a constant supply of nutrients during spring and summer. If you are using fertiliser in powder or granular form, water it in if no rain falls within 48 hours of its application.

Apply solutions of lawn feed through a hose dilutor. For small lawns, use a watering can and dilute the solution according to the manufacturer's instructions on the label.

Moss control

To control moss successfully, you must tackle the underlying causes such as shade, compacted soil and poor drainage. Moss can also build up in wet winters on otherwise healthy lawns and, if left untreated, it will smother and eventually kill the grass. The use of a lawn sand, that is a combined moss and weedkiller with added fertiliser, saves time and is ideal for the busy gardener. As this product feeds the grass, it will recover quickly and grow over the gaps left by the dead moss.

Apply the product on a day when there is heavy dew so that the chemicals stick to the moss and weed leaves. The moss and other weeds will turn black within five to seven days, but wait until the moss turns brown, which indicates that it is dead, before raking. Any patches that return to green should be treated again. Collect and dispose of the dead moss, but not in the compost bin, because the chemical residues will taint its contents.

Dealing with thatch

Over the year small quantities of grass clippings build up in the lawn, even when a collecting box is used. Grass blades die and lie on the soil, as do fragments of moss. If this debris is left it will form a layer of dead material called 'thatch', which often goes unnoticed. The most obvious indicator of thatch is when the lawn feels springy underfoot.

Scarifying, or raking, is the equivalent of giving an established lawn a good scrub and brush up. Use a wire rake to drag out all the thatch, dead grass and dead moss. For large lawns a powered scarifier simplifies this job. Once the debris is removed, air circulates more freely around the grass blades and water can penetrate to the roots.

TIP Don't scarify a new lawn, even one that has been turfed, because the vigorous action will cause damage.

Controlling moss

1 Use lawn sand at the rate recommended by the manufacturer, scattering it evenly on the lawn.
2 All brown, dead moss and debris should be removed with a fan-shaped wire rake. In case any moss is still alive, work from the edges of the area towards the centre to prevent it spreading.
3 Spike the soil in spring to aerate the grass roots so that they can breathe. This will help to reduce the growth of moss, which is most likely to develop in shady, wet conditions.

The protected environment of a greenhouse makes it possible to overwinter plants and sow early. During April and May there is a change of emphasis from keeping plants warm and safe from frost, to protecting them from sudden and extreme heat, as well as a marked increase in watering.

Spring checklist

■ **Gradually increase watering** as temperatures rise. Pots and trays can dry out rapidly on warm days, so keep some old newspapers handy to shade seedlings in bright weather.

■ **Ventilate the greenhouse** more freely, especially on still, sunny days, but remember to close the vents at night as temperatures are still low.

■ **Check heaters** are working efficiently before seeds start to germinate.

■ **Keep insulation in place** for a few more weeks. If it is very warm, remove fixed insulation cautiously but keep newspapers and fleece handy for sudden cold spells.

■ **Many pests start to appear** in spring so monitor plants carefully and guard against diseases such as damping-off.

■ **Sow any seeds** that you have saved at the appropriate time, after checking that they are still in good condition (see page 53).

■ **Continue sowing** annual bedding plants and hardy annuals (see page 18).

■ **Prick out seedlings** as soon as they can be handled easily (see page 18).

■ **Pot up rooted cuttings** that have overwintered under glass.

■ **Pot on rootbound plants** when they show signs of new growth (see opposite).

■ **Leave vents open wide** on milder days, to allow pollinating insects, such as bees and flies, to get into the greenhouse.

■ **Tie up the new shoots** of any climbing plants as they emerge.

■ **Revive tender perennials** by cutting out the less healthy looking stems and by repotting (see opposite).

■ **Propagate tender succulents** such as aeoniums and kalanchoes by taking cuttings from new sideshoots (see page 52).

■ **Take cuttings of begonias,** chrysanthemums, dahlias and gloxinias forced in winter, when their shoots are about 8cm (3in) long.

■ **Cut the blooms of *Anemone coronaria*** that were forced over winter for the house; continue to water and feed plants when flowering finishes.

■ **Liquid-feed greenhouse pot plants** such as calceolarias and cinerarias as they come into flower.

■ **Pot up lily bulbs** for early flowers. Plant out those that have flowered, after feeding and hardening off.

■ **Pot up lily-of-the-valley** for fragrant indoor blooms.

■ **Shield plants** from hot sunshine as the days lengthen and temperatures rise, to protect their leaves from drying and scorching; use shade paint on the glass or lower any blinds.

■ **On warmer days** increase humidity by soaking or 'damping down' the greenhouse floor and benches with a watering can or hose whenever you water your plants.

■ **Water and feed plants** regularly; it becomes critical at this time of year.

■ **Mulch greenhouse beds** with well-rotted organic matter or composted bark to prevent the soil from drying out quickly. If you have any plants in large pots, lay a mulch of gravel or shingle on the top of the compost to help keep roots moist.

■ **Harden off** all plants grown under glass, especially half-hardy kinds, which must be accustomed to cooler temperatures before being planted in the garden (see page 54).

■ **Pot up large seedlings** such as sunflowers and chrysanthemums individually, and move them on to the next pot size when their roots reach the sides.

Reviving tender plants

1 Tidy up any plants looking a bit worse for wear. Cut back leggy stems to promote new growth.
2 Carefully remove the plant from its pot, then tease out the roots with a pencil or plant label.

3 Using a larger pot, position the plant and then fill the space round the sides with new compost.
4 Use a cane to pack the compost down the sides, and then water carefully.

■ **Pot up mail-order plants** as they arrive and stand in a well-lit position. Keep them separate from your other plants for a few days in case they are carrying pests or diseases. Transfer seedlings and plug plants to trays or small pots as soon as possible.

■ **Watch out for the first signs** of aphids on the soft growth of fuchsias, carnations and other bedding plants, and vine weevil damage on many pot plants.

■ **Lightly spray the underside of leaves** with water in hot weather, to deter red spider mites from getting established.

■ **Inspect woody-stemmed plants** such as grape vines for scale insects.

■ **Take soft-tip cuttings** (see page 39), using short sideshoots or the growing tips of tender perennials, such as coleus, fuchsias, pelargoniums, marguerites, heliotropes and dahlias; flowering shrubs, such as hydrangeas, brooms and azaleas, and woody herbs like lemon verbena or sage.

■ **Take leaf cuttings** from begonias, african violets, gloxinias and streptocarpus (see pages 100–01).

Potting on a root-bound shrub

1 Select a pot, and then spread a layer of gravel or crocks in the bottom to aid drainage. Cover with a little compost. Position the plant in the centre, still in its pot, and then add or remove compost until the rims are level. Remove the smaller pot by twisting it, which should leave behind a neatly moulded hole.
2 Tap the base of the pot to remove the plant, position it in the hole and settle it in place by patting or knocking the pot on the staging. Water from above to consolidate the compost.

Propagation

This is the prime time for sowing seeds. The basic technique is the same for most flowers, although the amount of heat and light individual species require may differ. Always read the instructions on the packet. Take cuttings of soft shoots from succulents. If you have a cool or unheated greenhouse, use a heated propagator.

Sowing techniques You can sow seeds indoors in trays, modular trays, pans or small pots (see opposite). Make sure they are scrupulously clean and use fresh seed compost. After sowing, place the container in a propagator or cover it with a sheet of glass to prevent the compost from drying out. Remove this following germination. The following flowers and vegetables can be raised from seed in late spring.

■ **Grow cinerarias and primulas** (those grown under glass, such as *Primula obconica*, *P. sinensis* and *P. x kewensis*) in pots for early indoor colour from late winter.

■ **Sow late-flowering annuals** like china asters, chrysanthemums and zinnias.

■ **Sow fast-growing half-hardy annuals,** such as french marigolds (*Tagetes*), for bedding out in summer.

■ **Biennials and perennials** can be sown under glass if you have no space outdoors.

Cuttings of succulents Aeoniums, echeverias and kalanchoes that have been kept dry through winter can be watered to plump up their leaves and start them growing. Branching kinds, like *Aeonium arboreum*, often produce sideshoots that root easily to make vigorous new plants. Water and keep in a warm place out of full sun until rooted. If you want lots of plants, insert individual leaves (those you removed from the stems) in a tray of gritty compost and place this in a propagator.

Propagators These provide the right amount of warmth for germinating seeds or rooting cuttings. Some propagators are

Keep your greenhouse well ventilated as the days begin to lengthen and temperatures rise. Water plants well to ensure healthy growth.

Sowing seeds

1 Put more moist seed compost than you need in the seed tray and level it off with a piece of board.

2 Using a tamping board, press lightly to firm the compost and level the surface.

3 Do not pour seeds from the packet. Instead, place them in one hand and sprinkle them evenly and sparingly across the surface of the compost.

4 Sieve a thin layer of compost over the surface if the seeds need to be grown in darkness. Spray with a mist of water or stand the tray in shallow water to soak it up until the surface is moist.

5 The seedlings can be pricked out into trays or individual pots as soon as they are large enough to handle. This gives them space to grow.

shaped like small coldframes, others are trays with clear lids. More sophisticated models have a thermostatically controlled heating element and perhaps a misting unit.

You can make your own propagator by constructing a box on the greenhouse staging, topped with a clear, hinged lid. For additional heat, buy a soil-heating cable of adequate wattage for the temperature range you require, and lay this in a bed of horticultural sand at the bottom of the case. Fit a thermostat, with the control box on the outside, together with a maximum-minimum thermometer to monitor temperatures.

Alternatively, buy a propagating tray with a self-contained heating element and capillary mat for watering. Stand containers

Build a box with a hinged lid of glass or clear plastic and place it on the greenhouse staging to use as a propagator. Run a soil-heating cable along the bottom of the box and cover with horticultural sand to provide bottom heat.

of seeds or cuttings on the tray and cover them with plastic domes or the clear top supplied. Narrow windowsill models are also available for holding two to five seed trays.

Controlling temperature

Smell the air when you open the greenhouse doors. A good growing atmosphere is moist and earthy, whereas low humidity smells dry and dusty. There are several ways of keeping a greenhouse cool and moist.

■ **Use shade paint** and remember to apply it to the outside of the glass; shading the inside keeps out sunlight without reducing the temperature.

■ **Open ventilators** when temperatures rise much above 13°C (55°F) during the day; open wider on the lee of the greenhouse to prevent draughts from the windy side. Leave the door open in warm, still conditions.

■ **Leave vents open a little** at night as temperatures rise towards the end of spring.

■ **Improve the flow** of cool air by adding louvred panels to the greenhouse sides.

■ **Install automatic window openers,** adjusted to open once a chosen temperature is reached.

TIP If an unseasonable cold frosty night should threaten, place a covering of newspaper or fleece over seedlings and tender plants, and remove it in the morning.

After watering your plants it is worth spending a few minutes damping down the floor and benches. This reduces the temperature and increases humidity, which helps plants by reducing the amount of moisture lost through their leaves.

Shading plants from hot sun

Bright sunshine will scorch young seedlings, dry out compost and reduce humidity to levels at which plants struggle to grow healthily. Provide shade from April onwards with a special shade paint that becomes transparent in wet weather. Wash the greenhouse glass before applying a first, light coat to the outside of the glass with a roller, brush or spray. Follow with a denser second coat in late May. Alternatively, cover the greenhouse roof with shade netting, sold in various densities, or fit adjustable blinds that can be operated by hand or controlled automatically.

TIP Most greenhouses are inadequately ventilated, so consider adding more roof vents if you are finding it difficult to keep your greenhouse cool. Ideally, the total area of roof vents should equal 15 to 20 per cent of the ground area of the greenhouse.

Ready for the garden

The best way to acclimatise plants to outdoor conditions (harden off) is to transfer them to a coldframe and keep the lid closed for a week. If frost threatens, cover the frame overnight with a blanket or old carpet. Start ventilating the frame on mild days by raising the lid a little; gradually open it farther until it is left off completely after two to three weeks, when plants will be fully acclimatised.

An alternative is to stand plants outdoors on warm days, out of the wind, and bring them back in at night for the first two weeks. Leave them out for a few nights in succession before finally transplanting them into open ground.

Coldframes protect plants during extreme weather conditions and allow you to extend the growing season by several weeks (right).

Watering greenhouse plants

Greenhouse plants need good care to thrive. In hot or windy weather, all plants will need more water than when conditions are dull, cool or humid. Leafy, tropical and actively growing species require more water than cool or dry-climate plants, such as desert cacti and alpines.

■ **Established pot plants** should be checked at least once daily; they will need more water as the days become warmer.

■ **The best time to water** is first thing in the morning or late in the afternoon. Avoid wetting the foliage in bright sunlight, as it could scorch.

■ **Keep water in a tank** if there is room so it remains at greenhouse temperature. Alternatively, fill a couple of cans with mains water and leave them in the greenhouse overnight to warm up.

■ **Stand young seedlings** and dry plants in a tray of water (right). When they have soaked up as much as they require, allow them to drain.

Summer

The mainstay of the summer border, this is the time to increase the display by planting less hardy varieties for guaranteed colour through to autumn. Keep plants at their best by staking, thinning out and deadheading and, with an eye to the future, take a few cuttings of tender perennials.

Summer checklist

■ **Plant tender perennials** as early as possible so they establish quickly and start flowering, but make sure they are hardened off over a couple of weeks.

■ **Perennials raised from seed** in spring can be potted up into a minimum pot size of 8cm (3in) once they are well rooted.

■ **Water newly planted perennials** in dry spells. Soak them every few days, so water penetrates right through the rootball and roots are encouraged to reach down in search of moisture.

■ **Deadhead faded flowers** to prevent their seed from setting.

■ **Thin overcrowded clumps** of perennials to increase air circulation and prevent the stems from flopping over. Cut out a quarter to a third of the stems at ground level.

■ **Stake tall-growing perennials,** including late-flowering cimicifugas, michaelmas daisies and phlox, before they begin to flop; once this happens, stems will never straighten properly (see page 60). Surround clumps with a ring of short stakes and run garden string around the stakes. 'Grow-through' plant supports give the best results, but need to be in place early.

■ **Hoe and hand-weed borders** every couple of weeks. Hoeing off weeds as they germinate saves the more difficult job of tackling large, established weeds later on. Look for larger weeds that may be growing unnoticed among mature perennials, and pull them up before they seed. Bindweed and ground elder are a real nuisance once established – treat them with a weedkiller or dig up every scrap of root.

Echinacea's large, daisy-like flowers – seen here attracting a painted lady butterfly – produce a striking display in the late summer border.

Cutting back untidy perennials

1 Perennials such as geraniums become straggly and untidy when they have finished blooming. To tidy the flowerbed and encourage new growth, cut them back to ground level using shears.

2 Any straggly stems remaining can be cut off neatly, then all the trimmings should be cleared up and placed on the compost heap. Leaving rotting stems is untidy and could attract disease.

3 Once the ground is tidy, apply a sprinkling of general fertiliser and then water well. It won't take long for the plant to develop a tidy mound of fresh foliage and usually more flowers.

■ **Protect hostas** from slugs and snails throughout summer. Try growing them in large pots to keep these pests at bay.

■ **Avoid powdery mildew** on susceptible perennials, such as phlox and pulmonarias, by watering well during dry spells.

■ **Pick off leaves** affected by fungal disease and throw them away – do not put them on the compost heap. Plants prone to infection include aquilegias, phlox and pulmonarias. Consider spraying with fungicide to prevent diseases from spreading.

■ **Propagate some perennials** by cuttings or division (see page 61).

■ **Deadhead border perennials** regularly to improve their looks and prolong their display until the first frosts.

■ **Cut back perennials** that have finished flowering and are flopping over, such as catmint (*Nepeta*), achilleas and hardy geraniums (see above).

■ **Water and feed** perennials grown in containers regularly. Keep new plants moist by watering thoroughly every couple of days if necessary. Established perennials that are not drought tolerant will benefit from a good soaking twice a week during prolonged periods of dry weather.

■ **Keep a look out** for pests and diseases, including slugs and snails, aphids, vine weevil grubs – which attack the roots of container-grown plants – and fungal problems such as mildew.

■ **Plant new perennials** for autumn flowers (see page 60).

■ **Feed tender perennials** and plants that are coming up to flowering with a high-potash liquid fertiliser.

■ **Pot up rooted cuttings** taken earlier and thin seedlings.

■ **Propagate new perennials** by layering (see page 140) and by taking cuttings (see page 61).

■ **Prepare the ground** for autumn planting.

■ **Divide established clumps** of the earliest spring-flowering perennials (see page 63 and page 107).

■ **Collect seed** for sowing or storing; pot up any self-sown seedlings you wish to keep over the winter.

Planting and transplanting

■ **Fill gaps in your border** with autumn-flowering perennials. They will make a handsome display this year provided you buy large plants in 15–20cm (6–8in) pots. Choose bushy, well-grown specimens with plenty of flower buds and avoid any that are tall, leggy or yellow leaved.

■ **Plant out young perennials** that have been raised from seed or cuttings earlier in the year, so long as the roots are well developed in a minimum pot size of 8cm (3in). Alternatively, pot them on into 13cm (5in) pots ready to plant out next year.

■ **Transplant or pot up** young perennials that have self-seeded in the border or on gravel paths. It is worth looking out for such seedlings before hoeing or spraying the areas with weedkiller. Either pot up plants into 8cm (3in) pots or grow them in a row in a nursery bed or on a spare piece of ground and plant out next year.

■ **Plan new borders** and prepare the ground for planting hardy herbaceous perennials. At the very end of summer, the soil is warm and moist, which encourages plenty of root growth, while the shorter days and falling temperatures ensure that the plants do not put their energies into making excess top growth.

Euphorbias make dramatic feature plants in the garden. Cut shoots that have flowered to ground level when they start to fade, wearing gloves to do this as the milky sap can cause irritation.

Staking

It is essential to stake tall-growing perennials early in summer before they topple. Once they have flopped over, the stems will not grow straight. Use ready-made frames, canes or twiggy sticks, staking individual stems of very tall plants, like those of delphiniums.

■ **Tailor-made supports** vary in style and are reusable. Many can be raised as the plants grow or may be interlinked to support clumps of different sizes.

■ **Place short canes in a circle** round the plant, with string run round and in between.

■ **Poke in twiggy branches of hazel,** often referred to as 'pea sticks', round a perennial clump. If bent over at the top, these sticks will make a cage through which the plant will be able to grow.

■ **Bamboo canes and soft string** or raffia provide reliable support for tall, individual perennial stems.

Deadheading

Removing dead or faded flowerheads encourages more blooms. If this job is neglected, plants will set seed and flower less freely. With regular deadheading, tender perennials will flower well into autumn.

■ **Self-seeding perennials,** such as lady's mantle (*Alchemilla mollis*) and bronze fennel

(*Foeniculum vulgare* 'Purpureum'), can produce many seedlings informally throughout a border. If you want this to happen, leave the flowerheads in place to allow the seeds to ripen; if not, remove flowerheads as they fade.

■ **Spring and early** summer-flowering perennials such as hardy geraniums and oriental poppies (*Papaver orientale*) should be cut back to ground level once they have finished flowering. Feed them with a general fertiliser and water in well, and they will soon reward you with a bushy mound of fresh foliage.

■ **Deadhead peonies,** but allow the foliage to die back naturally.

■ **For delphiniums and lupins** cut off dead flower spikes to encourage more flowers on shorter sideshoots.

Propagation

Summer is the perfect time to make more plants by taking a variety of cuttings, by dividing and through collecting seeds.

Although spring is far away, now is also the time to divide polyanthus to ensure a good show of flowers next year.

Cuttings Take soft-tip cuttings to propagate woody-based tender perennials (see below) and varieties of herbaceous perennials that are difficult or impossible to raise from seed or division – these include penstemon and phygelius. Most tender perennials root easily from cuttings that are taken during summer, though with non-woody herbaceous perennials it is important to select non-flowering shoots.

Take cuttings in the cool of the morning. Select strong, non-flowering shoots and cut a length of stem 10cm (4in) long from the top. Put the cut material straight into a plastic bag or bucket of cold water to prevent it from wilting. A high level of humidity is important for success, so either cover the pots with an inflated clear polythene bag secured with an elastic band or place them in a propagator out of the sun. The

---

Taking soft-tip cuttings

1 To make the cuttings, use a sharp knife and trim the base just below a leaf joint.

2 Using the knife, take off the lower leaves and any flowers carefully.

3 The base of each cutting should then be dipped into hormone rooting powder before it is inserted round the edge of a 13cm (5in) pot

filled with cuttings compost. To create humidity, cover the pot with a polythene bag and place it in a shaded coldframe or sheltered spot outside. (Do not cover pelargoniums, which can rot.) Rooting usually takes about eight weeks, at which point the cuttings should be potted up individually into 8cm (3in) pots.

exception here is pelargoniums, which are prone to rotting and so best left uncovered.

After about eight weeks, carefully remove the pot to check whether the roots are well developed. If they are, pot up the cuttings individually into 8cm (3in) pots. Overwinter the young plants on a windowsill or in a greenhouse; the parent plant can be left to take its chances outside.

Take basal cuttings of clump-forming perennials, such as lupins and delphiniums, before the end of June. Cut strong, young shoots about 10cm (4in) long from the base of the plant and treat them as described for soft-tip cuttings (see page 61).

Plant out basal cuttings taken in late spring in a nursery bed, or move them into individual 8cm (3in) pots and grow them on in a coldframe or sheltered area of the garden.

Propagate pinks (*Dianthus*) from 'pipings' – these are tips of non-flowering shoots that have been pulled out. After removing the lower leaves, treat as soft-tip cuttings (see page 61).

Layering border carnations
Select non-flowering sideshoots for layering, then improve the soil around the plant by forking in a quantity of potting compost where the layer is to root.

■ **Use a knife to remove a small sliver,** about 1cm (½in) long, from the underside of a sideshoot; the wound will stimulate root production. Peg the wounded area of the stem into the soil using a bent wire.

■ **Stake the end of the shoot** to keep it upright. Lightly cover the wounded area of the plant with soil.

■ **Layers should be well rooted** by autumn, when they can be detached and moved to a nursery bed, then planted out next year.

Propagating by division
While most perennials are divided in autumn or spring, those that bloom early in spring, like bleeding heart (*Dicentra spectabilis*),

Pulmonaria can be divided easily. Lift a clump with a fork and pull it apart into smaller pieces or individual plantlets. Discard the old central portion and replant the divisions. Water the plants well and keep them moist in dry weather.

leopard's bane (*Doronicum*) and pulmonaria do better if you divide them in late August or early September. By waiting until late summer, they have enough time to establish themselves before flowering next year. This easy method of propagation also rejuvenates old plants that have formed large, congested clumps (see above).

■ **Divide polyanthus** and double-flowered primulas after flowering. Dig up the clump with a fork and shake off any loose soil. Use a sharp knife to cut the clump into smaller pieces, each consisting of one or two shoots with plenty of roots attached to it. Plant out the divisions in rows, in either a nursery bed or a spare corner of the garden, spacing them 15–23cm (6–9in) apart. Water them well.

■ **Split the rhizomes** of bearded irises in established clumps once flowering has finished (see opposite). Replant the divisions in full sunlight.

Raising from seed You can raise many hardy perennials from seed, either those you have purchased or those you have collected yourself. Bear in mind when collecting seed that although the offspring of plant species come true, those of cultivated varieties are likely to be variable and often inferior to the parent plant.

Gather seed of spring and early summer-flowering perennials as soon as it is ripe, usually when the seed pods have turned brown. On a dry day cut the seed heads into labelled paper bags and place on a sunny windowsill. Once the seed heads are completely dry, tip them onto a sheet of newspaper, split open the pods and shake out the seed. Store in envelopes or empty film canisters; do not use polythene bags as the seeds could rot. Label each container with the plant name and the date.

The seed of most perennials can be sown immediately, but a few, such as aconitums, meconopsis and primulas, need a cold period in order to germinate, and they should be left until autumn. The best place to store seed for any length of time is in moisture-proof containers in a refrigerator or other cool, dry place.

When you are ready, sow the collected seed thinly into pots of moist seed compost and cover with a thin layer of perlite or horticultural vermiculite. Stand the pots in a coldframe or other sheltered spot outside, and keep the compost moist. Alternatively, sow seeds outside in rows in a well-cultivated nursery bed.

Helping seed germination Most perennials are suitable for sowing immediately, but certain varieties need special treatment in order to germinate. The seeds of baptisia and lupin have a hard coating that needs to be chipped carefully with a sharp knife or rubbed with sandpaper to allow water to penetrate before germination can take place. Others, such as certain varieties of campanula and

Dividing bearded irises

1 Using a fork, lift the clump. Cut off the younger outer pieces of rootstock, or rhizome, and discard the old central portion.

2 To prevent strong winds from buffeting the plants, trim the leaves.

3 The irises should be replanted in groups of three, with the fans of foliage facing to the outside. The top of the rhizome must be just above soil level, as it needs exposure to sun in order to flower well. Feed with a low-nitrogen fertiliser and water thoroughly.

primula, require a cold period, known as stratification. To stratify seeds, mix them with damp potting compost in a plastic bag and keep in the fridge for several weeks, then sow in autumn.

The flower garden becomes a celebration of colour as summer annuals take over from spring bedding. Continue sowing to prolong your display and deadheading to keep plants flowering into autumn. Let some set seed for sowing next season and also bring on new plants for next spring.

Summer checklist

■ **Finish hardening off tender annuals,** such as scarlet salvias and busy lizzies (*Impatiens*), and plant them out as soon as the frosts are over. Use them in formal and informal bedding schemes.

■ **Give a weekly liquid feed** to pots and trays of bedding plants, and to other seedlings that will flower, if their planting out has been delayed. A high-potash fertiliser, such as a tomato feed, can be used every seven to 14 days.

Hollyhocks will thrive for several years if cut down to 15cm (6in) after flowering.

■ **Water recently planted bedding** and transplanted seedlings regularly during dry weather. All plants should be watered regularly during summer, but pay special attention to those growing in containers.

■ **Water and feed sweet peas** at regular intervals, and deadhead to prevent seeds from forming. Tie in the stems every two or three days when growing up vertical string supports as a cordon.

■ **Buy seedlings and plug plants** from the garden centre (see opposite).

■ **Cut flowers for drying,** such as statice (*Limonium sinuatum*), helichrysum and helipterum (*Rhodanthe*). Sown in March and April, they will start to flower in July when you can cut the earliest young blooms to dry as everlasting flowers.

■ **Transplant biennials** sown outdoors last month to a spare piece of ground, where they can mature until the autumn (see opposite).

■ **Pot up individual seedlings,** each in a 5–8cm (2–3in) pot, to make eye-catching feature plants for larger containers.

■ **Thin seedlings,** such as love-in-a-mist (*Nigella damascena*), sown in late spring where they are to flower, to 5–10cm (2–4in) apart according to vigour. Discard spare seedlings, or carefully transplant them and water immediately (see opposite).

■ **Keep weeding,** especially in beds of densely planted annuals where weeds can flower and self-seed unnoticed. If possible, do this without treading on the soil between flowering plants.

■ **Sow fast-growing annuals** such as candytuft (*Iberis*), linaria, night-scented stock and annual chrysanthemums. They will provide a display in autumn if sown now, either where they are to flower or grown in a spare piece of ground for transplanting later.

■ **Sow spring-flowering biennials,** especially brompton stocks (*Matthiola incana*), forget-me-nots and dwarf varieties of wallflowers. Start them off now in a spare bed, then plant out in early autumn.

■ **Clear away** exhausted spring bedding. Weed and lightly fork the soil, and rake in a dressing of fertiliser. The bed is then ready for summer planting.

■ **Protect young annuals** from slugs and snails, removing these pests by hand. Also watch out for signs of seasonal problems such as moulds, mildews and virus diseases, earwigs and red spider mites, and vine weevils, which attack the roots of plants growing in containers. Deter red spider mites, which strike in hot, dry weather, by misting plants with water.

■ **Feed annuals in containers** with a high-potash fertiliser, such as tomato feed – every seven to ten days.

■ **Deadhead annuals,** such as pansies, marigolds, snapdragons and California poppies, to stimulate more flowers. Remove all faded flowers to prolong the display, unless you intend saving the seeds. Allow the best annuals to set seed then, when they are ripe, gather and dry to store.

■ **Fill gaps in your display** by planting late-sown annuals, and water them in with a diluted liquid feed.

■ **Support tall flowers** such as sunflowers and hollyhocks before their stalks bend, and continue tying in sweet peas and other annual climbers.

■ **Lower cordon sweet peas** that have reached the top of their canes (see page 67).

■ **Sow some hardy annuals** at the end of summer. These will overwinter and flower early next year (see page 67).

■ **Encourage bushy growth** by cutting back by half the long bare stems of sprawling annuals, such as petunias, and by pinching out the tips of long shoots of helichrysums and nasturtiums.

Buying seedlings

If you are not able to sow your own seeds, you can buy plug plants from a garden centre. If the weather is warm enough, plant them straight out, or transplant into individual pots where they can be kept for two weeks before planting them in the ground. Scattering a layer of horticultural grit on the soil in coldframes deters pests and keeps the soil surface dry, thus eliminating moss.

Transplanting biennials

By July, seedlings of biennials such as wallflowers, forget-me-nots and foxgloves (*Digitalis*) sown during late spring will be

Transplanting seedlings

1 Seedlings sown in seedbeds or trays in late spring should now be pricked out as they will need much more space to develop. Tease them apart gently, handling them carefully by the leaves so that you do not damage their roots. If they are really entangled, place a clump of seedlings with their soil in a large bowl of water; this should make them much easier to separate.

2 The sturdiest of the seedlings can be moved straight to their final flowering position, but the smaller ones, like these, are best grown on in a spare bed until they are larger. They will respond well to a warm, sheltered, sunny position; make sure that they never dry out.

clamouring for extra space. Now is the time to thin them out.

■ **Do this in the bed,** first to 5cm (2in) apart and later to 10–20cm (4–8in).

■ **For larger, sturdier plants,** transplant them to a spare, lightly shaded bed that has been forked over with added compost and a dressing of general fertiliser. Plant them in rows 23cm (9in) apart. Space hollyhocks (*Alcea*), foxgloves and other large plants 20cm (8in) apart, most other biennials 10–15cm (4–6in) apart. Pinch out the tips of wallflowers to encourage branching. Water them in well and keep moist during spells of dry weather.

Planting formal bedding

Most flowers used for formal, organised summer bedding schemes are slightly tender and cannot be safely planted outdoors until early summer, after being hardened off for a week or two. In an informal bedding scheme the flowers are planted in natural-looking groups and drifts. Work out your colour scheme, and the patterns or shapes you want to create, before preparing the ground.

■ **Clear the ground** of any previous bedding and weeds, lightly fork it over and spread a dressing of granular or powdered general fertiliser. Rake this in, level the bed and remove any stones.

■ **First plant the tall 'dot' plants,** which dominate and catch the eye, where they will be the focus of the display, singly or in small groups, spaced about 1m (3ft) apart. Good examples include fuchsias, heliotropes and pelargoniums grown as standards, as well as cannas, cordylines, castor-oil plants (*Ricinus communis*) and variegated maize.

■ **Then plant the edging,** using dwarf flowers spaced about 10–15cm (4–6in) apart. Try white alyssum, lobelia, marigolds, silver-leaved cinerarias (*Senecio cineraria*) and dwarf phlox.

■ **Fill the space in between** with flowers of intermediate height, spaced 23–30cm

Tidy pot marigolds (*Calendula*) and remove faded flowers to stimulate a second blooming, keeping the garden colourful well into autumn.

(9–12in) apart, depending on size and vigour. Good plants include bedding dahlias, coleus, pelargoniums, petunias and salvias.

■ **Water in well after planting,** adding a liquid fertiliser to give plants a flying start.

Deadheading

Some annuals will cease flowering once they have set their first seeds, so it is important to deadhead pansies, petunias and antirrhinums if you want them to continue into the autumn. Others, such as tagetes, begonias and impatiens, are either 'self-cleaning', dropping their faded flowers naturally, or are unaffected by seed development. For these, deadheading is unnecessary, as it is for those special plants you have selected for saving seed.

Collecting seeds

Many flowers start to set seeds from midsummer. Collect the seeds of superior or unusual annuals for sowing next season – but not from F1 hybrids, which rarely come true. Gather the seed heads before they are fully ripe and start shedding their seed.

■ **When the seed heads look dry** or start to change colour, cut them off carefully and invert them into paper bags.

■ **Tie the bags around the stems** and hang them upside down in a dry, airy place to finish ripening.

■ **After a week or two,** shake out the dry seeds, gently blow away the chaff and store them in labelled envelopes in an airtight tin away from extreme cold and heat.

Sowing annuals for next year

Although most hardy annuals are sown in spring, many produce larger, stronger plants if they are sown in late summer and early autumn, and will flower earlier next year. This can help to bridge the gap between spring and summer bedding.

Sow them outdoors *in situ* in mild areas, or in rows in a spare piece of ground where they can be covered with cloches or fleece in very cold weather. Thin the seedlings to 8–10cm (3–4in) apart when they are large enough to handle. Alternatively, start them under glass, prick out into trays or individual small pots, and keep these in a coldframe over winter.

Lowering sweet peas

Sweet peas growing up individual vertical supports often have several more weeks flowering left after they reach the tops of their tall canes. The plants flower mostly at the top of their stems rather than along their length, so to prolong flowering, remove them from their canes and re-attach them to adjacent ones.

■ **Carefully untie each stem** and lay it neatly along the ground from its original cane to the next cane in the row. Re-attach the top 30–45cm (12–18in) of the stem to this new cane.

■ **Continue to do this with** all the other sweet pea plants, moving them along the row to the next cane. The first cane will need to be moved to the end of the row.

■ **Continue watering** and feeding regularly. Control slugs and cut flowers before they can set seed.

Cut sweet peas, such as *Lathyrus* 'Violet Queen', regularly. They make a scented display indoors, and the more you cut the more you will get.

Summer is a busy bulb season. Spring bulbs will require dividing or storing, the new season's bulbs need tending, and autumn-flowering bulbs should be planted. Towards late summer, start to plan next spring's display as well as establishing pots to force for winter enjoyment indoors.

Summer checklist

■ **Lift, dry and store** hyacinths, tulips, daffodils and other spring-flowering bulbs that are dying down by early August. Store them in a cool, dry place until planting time.

■ **Dig up and divide** overcrowded clumps of daffodils (see page 70), once their foliage has died down, and clumps of other bulbs that failed to flower in spring. Discard them if they show signs of disease.

■ **Plant autumn bulbs** such as colchicums, saffron (*Crocus sativus*) and crocuses, as well as *Amaryllis belladonna* 5–8cm (2–3in) deep, close to a warm, sunny wall.

■ **Plant out begonias** grown from tubers or cuttings taken in late spring and dahlias grown from seed or cuttings (then mulch).

■ **Arum lilies** that have flowered indoors should be planted out to rest, standing those grown in pots outdoors in a shallow pool.

■ **Feed summer-flowering bulbs** planted in pots while they are in bloom and for three to four weeks afterwards, and keep moist.

■ **Water recently planted bulbs** during a dry spell, especially those in containers or close to walls, and species such as galtonias and gladioli. A light mulch after watering helps to keep the ground moist.

■ **Stake large-flowered gladioli** in windy gardens. If being grown for cut flowers, cut the spikes low down the stem when the bottom flower is almost fully open and feed plants every seven to 14 days with a high-potash fertiliser to encourage more blooms.

Allium hollandicum **'Purple Sensation'** has hemispherical heads of purple flowers. The dried seed heads are valued in floral arrangements.

Naturalising bulbs in grass

1 Using a spade, cut a large 'H' in the turf. Under-cut the turf from the middle and peel back two panels to expose a rectangle of soil. Use a fork to loosen the soil underneath.

2 Dig in bone meal at a rate of 15g per m² (½oz per sq yd). Distribute the bulbs randomly over the exposed soil, ensuring they are at least 2–3cm (1in) apart. Press each one in gently.

3 Before carefully replacing the turf, make sure all the bulbs are pointing upwards. Firm the turf gently with your hand and, if necessary, fill the joints between the turf with fine soil.

■ **Watch for pests and diseases,** especially ailments such as narcissus eelworm, which causes stunting, and lily viruses, signalled by failed flowers and mottled foliage.

■ **Reduce the water** given to amaryllis (*Hippeastrum*) in pots, to allow bulbs to rest.

■ **Hand-weed** between groups of lilies and other bulbs that seed freely, to keep them in large clumps and not let them spread.

■ **Sow bluebells** (*Hyacinthoides*) and other bulbs that grow well from seed, in trays or in a nursery bed.

■ **Deadhead late spring bulbs** as they fade – unless you want to grow more from seed. Sow collected seeds immediately in pots or trays, or outdoors in rows in a spare bed. Sow ripe lily seeds now, or keep them cold in the fridge and sow next spring.

■ **Deadhead and stake dahlias** and disbud for larger flowers (see page 71). Continue feeding regularly, using only high-potash feeds from mid-August onwards.

■ **Plan next spring's displays.** Bulbs such as daffodils benefit from being planted in August or September, so order them when the bulb catalogues appear from late August.

■ **Begin planting spring bulbs** outdoors, starting in late August with daffodils, muscari and erythroniums, followed in September with most other kinds. Tulips are best left until November (see page 110), as earlier planting encourages diseases such as tulip fire.

■ **Consider naturalising patches** of spring bulbs in your lawn (see above).

■ **Feed autumn-flowering bulbs** naturalised in grass with bone meal, applied once during August at 65g per m² (2oz per sq yd), or with a high-potash fertiliser at recommended rates.

■ **Pot up prepared bulbs** in early September to flower over Christmas and the New Year, as well as arum lilies for winter flowering under glass (see page 134).

■ **Collect lily bulbils** – dark, immature bulbs growing at the base of the leaves – and plant them 2–3cm (1in) apart in trays of compost in a coldframe or under glass.

Buying and planting bulbs

Whether you buy bulbs from a garden centre or by mail-order, plant them as soon as possible. Erythroniums, trilliums and other bulbs without a skin or 'tunic' should be kept in moist bark or compost.

The best flowers come from the biggest bulbs, so if your bulb catalogue offers a range of sizes, choose the largest you can afford. However, the lower grade or 'second-size' bulbs are more economical for naturalising in large quantities.

Distinguish between a mixture and a collection. A collection is a number of separate and labelled varieties sold at a discount. Mixtures can be good value but be prepared for an unpredictable range of colours. Inexpensive mixtures may comprise undersized bulbs and just common varieties.

If you prefer to buy loose and pre-packed bulbs in shops and garden centres, look for bulbs that are clean, firm and plump, with no obvious root or shoot growth. Avoid those that are dirty, soft, damaged, shrivelled or showing signs of mould or pale, forced shoots and roots. Be wary of bulbs kept in warm conditions, as they are more likely to be soft and actively growing.

Planting bulbs

Autumn-flowering bulbs provide a welcome late show of colour in beds, borders and containers. Plant them in July, 10cm (4in) deep, in informal groups. The soil should have been well forked over, and fed with plenty of garden compost or a high-potash fertiliser for good flowers.

■ **Colchicums have large mauve** or white, crocus-like blooms; the large leaves appear in spring. The best is *Colchicum speciosum*.

■ **Autumn crocuses** flower in shades of lilac, blue, purple and white. Leaves appear in spring. There are many terrific species, including *Crocus speciosus* and its varieties and the scented, lilac *C. goulimyi*.

■ **The brilliant, golden-yellow** crocus-like flowers of *Sternbergia lutea* appear in September and October, accompanied by dwarf, strap-shaped leaves.

Finish planting your daffodil bulbs by the end of August, as their roots start growing in late summer. However, there is usually no harm in waiting until September, the usual time for planting other spring-flowering bulbs (except for tulips). If you are planning a bedding display with wallflowers and other spring-flowering plants, you can even wait until early October in mild areas.

■ **Bulbs in borders** look more appealing flowering in informal groups rather than in symmetrical patterns. Before planting it is worth enriching a light soil with plenty of garden compost or well-rotted manure. If your soil is heavy, dig in some coarse sand or grit to improve drainage.

■ **Many smaller bulbs,** such as fritillaries, snowdrops or crocuses, add charming informality to areas of a lawn or wild garden, especially under deciduous trees.

■ **Before planting in grass** mow the area as short as possible. You must wait at least six weeks after flowering before mowing the grass, to allow the bulb foliage to die down naturally and ensure flowers in future years.

TIP You can plant dried tubers in late summer, 15cm (6in) apart and 2–3cm (1in) deep; they will take over a year to establish. A more reliable method is to buy 'green', or growing, plants in pots and plant them in well-drained soil in semi-shade.

Clumps of daffodils that have become overcrowded should be lifted with a fork once their foliage has died down. The clumps can be divided into smaller clusters and replanted immediately, or separated into individual bulbs and dried for storing.

Lifting, drying and dividing

Bedding hyacinths and most hybrid tulips need to be dug up and dried in summer to keep the bulbs in peak condition to replant in autumn. Daffodils benefit from being lifted every few years to prevent overcrowding and reduced flowering.

■ **Once foliage has died down**, carefully lift the bulbs with a fork; insert it well away to avoid spearing the bulbs.

■ **Rub off as much soil as possible**, then spread out the bulbs on trays or in shallow boxes lined with newspaper. When they are quite dry, with withered roots and papery skins, trim the roots and remove loose skin.

■ **Store the sound bulbs** in paper bags or boxes in a cool, dry place. Discard any damaged, soft or discoloured bulbs, as well as small, young bulblets.

TIP Many daffodil varieties have multiple 'noses' – small offset bulbs produced at the side of the parent. These can be left in place or carefully removed for storing until autumn, when you can plant them in rows in spare ground. Leave until they are larger and have reached flowering size.

Hardy cyclamen are excellent for naturalising in groups among trees or shrubs, thriving in sun or partial shade.

Under trees and hedges

Although most bulbs prefer to grow in full sun, some kinds are unaffected by, and even appreciate, the shade cast by deciduous trees and hedges. They have usually adapted to woodland conditions by producing flowers or foliage before the tree leaves open and cast shade, or by manufacturing food slowly and wilting if light and heat levels become too intense. Other bulbs grow happily anywhere, but their flowers often last longer out of bright sunshine.

■ **Before planting enrich the top** few centimetres of soil with moisture-retentive organic material such as garden compost or leaf-mould; add more every autumn.

■ **To relieve dense shade** thin branches unobtrusively to admit extra light and rain.

■ **Check the habits and preferences** of a particular variety – not all bulbs will perform well in shady or woodland conditions.

Disbudding a dahlia

Dahlias often produce smaller buds to each side of the main bud. Check your plants to see if they have produced any and, if so, remove them. By doing so, you channel the plant's energy into making fewer, larger flowers. Deadheading the faded blooms will also help to stimulate further flowering. If you have any dahlias still at the seedling stage, try pinching out their growing tips to produce bushy plants.

In summer, roses take centre stage. From late June onwards you can enjoy all the different kinds, including those that flower just once a year. Gather roses to brighten the house and deadhead those in the garden regularly to keep the plants flowering well into autumn.

Summer checklist

■ **Tie the stems** of young climbing and rambler roses temporarily to supports. This prevents wind damage and keeps the plants tidy. They can be secured permanently in late summer or autumn.

■ **Deadhead blooms as soon as they fade** (see below right), unless hips are required later in the season.

■ **Water newly planted roses** if the weather is dry for more than two weeks. Give each plant around 5 litres (2 gallons) of water. Established roses are deep-rooting and relatively drought-tolerant.

■ **Container-grown roses** need watering regularly, checking the compost daily during hot weather. Add a dilute liquid fertiliser every seven to 14 days.

■ **Apply a summer dressing** of rose fertiliser and lightly hoe or rake it in (see right). Do this soon after the longest day. Do not feed roses after the end of July.

■ **Disbud hybrid tea** and floribunda roses to encourage good-quality late blooms.

■ **Propagate your favourite varieties** from bud cuttings during July.

■ **Keep weeding,** especially around new roses. Hoe and hand-weed but avoid forking near plants in case you injure the roots and cause suckers to appear.

■ **Remove suckers immediately,** if they appear (see page 74).

■ **Spray a combined insecticide-fungicide** at fortnightly intervals if you wish, or need, to take preventative measures against a range of potential problems. In any event, watch out for signs of mildew, black spot, rust and aphids.

■ **Move roses in pots outdoors** so that they can rest after flowering. Stand them in a

Cultivated for over 4000 years, there are roses to suit every place and occasion – making them the world's most popular garden shrub.

sunny, sheltered place, or put each pot in a planting hole so that the compost will not dry out too rapidly.

■ **Cut blooms for indoors** from late June onwards. Remove only from established, strongly growing plants, and cut off no more than a third of the stem, with a sloping cut, just above an outward-facing bud.

■ **Harvest fragrant roses** at their best, then dry the petals in layers in a warm, airy room. Use them as the basis of a potpourri.

■ **Before going on holiday,** remove all fading and fully open flowers. This prevents hips from developing while you are away, wasting the plant's energy.

■ **Prune ramblers and weeping standards** from late August onwards (see page 75).

■ **Start taking hardwood cuttings** at the end of summer.

■ **Rust and red spider mite** are prevalent in late summer, so keep an eye out for them and continue preventative spraying.

■ **Plan new plantings,** order roses and start getting beds ready for autumn planting (see page 75).

■ **Cut off developing seed heads,** unless the hips are decorative.

■ **Check supports and ties are secure** on standard, pillar and arch-trained roses, before early autumn winds start to blow.

■ **Underplant roses** with hyacinth bulbs for excellent edging or underplanting.

Deadhead repeat-flowering roses regularly to encourage more blooms, using secateurs to make an outward, sloping cut.

Deadheading

The removal of faded blooms is a form of light pruning that prolongs flowering on repeat-flowering roses. It also stops roses from making seed, so do not deadhead species roses and once-flowering roses that produce attractive hips.

■ **Cut off complete floribunda trusses** with a good length of stem to prevent the bushes from producing thin, unproductive shoots.

■ **On hybrid tea roses** remove the faded blooms with a portion of the stem. Cut the stem two to three leaves down from the flower and just above a strong leaf bud. Never remove more than half the shoot because this can delay further flowering.

Disbudding roses

Disbudding is the best way to produce top-quality flowers. On hybrid tea varieties, cleanly pull off or pinch out the small buds that can form around a central bud. Do this as early as possible to divert the plant's energy into the single remaining flower and you will get large, fully formed blooms. Also, pinch out or snip off the central bud in the flower trusses of floribunda and modern shrub roses. This encourages the other buds to open together, creating a better, showier display, and it helps to reduce overcrowding.

Feeding roses

While it is not essential to feed roses to get a good display, they will be healthier and more resistant to disease if you do. Give all roses a summer dressing of high-potash or rose fertiliser, sprinkled evenly around the base of the plant. This is the second of two annual feeds (the first being in early spring), and should be given in the first half of July; later feeding causes soft growth, which will not ripen before autumn frosts.

TIP You can give young roses, and those growing on 'hungry', light soils, an additional liquid boost one month before the main summer feed. Apply onto the soil or spray as a foliar feed on a cloudy day when it will not immediately evaporate or scorch the leaves.

Removing suckers

Suckers growing from the rootstocks of grafted roses are usually conspicuous at this time of year because of their paler colour and smaller, more numerous leaflets. If left uncontrolled they can come to dominate the plant, so remove each one promptly.

■ **Trace the sucker** to where it joins the root and pull it off cleanly, wearing strong gardening gloves. Replace the soil and re-firm the rose in the ground (see below).

■ **Suckers on standard roses** sprout from the tall stem; remove any as soon as you spot them, using secateurs.

Late-summer pruning

By late summer, rambling roses have flowered and it is now the season to prune them (see right). Ramblers can be distinguished from climbing roses by their vigorous, pliable stems. They have small flowers that are borne in huge trusses, formed on new shoots. Ramblers come into flower just once a year, from early to mid summer, but generally produce a long display of abundant blooms.

■ **Do not prune ramblers** in their first year. From the second year onwards, remove two or three entire main stems every year. Cut back the remaining main stems by about one-quarter of their length and the sideshoots by two-thirds.

■ **The stems to be cut out** will be long and some ramblers bear particularly sharp thorns. You may find it easier, therefore, to cut out the chosen stems in small sections.

Weeping standard roses are also pruned in late summer. Remove as much of the older growth as possible and leave the best of this year's growth as replacement.

Taking hardwood cuttings

The majority of roses are propagated commercially by budding. This delicate operation joins a bud from a chosen variety onto a wild rose root system (rootstock). This technique requires a lot of skill. Gardeners, therefore, tend to prefer easier methods such as using cuttings, or layering for climbers and ramblers.

Most roses – except hybrid teas – can be grown from hardwood cuttings. These root easily and the resulting plants grow on their own roots, so there will be no problem with suckers. Take the cuttings between late August and early October, selecting strong, well-ripened stems about the thickness of a pencil.

■ **Cut off and discard** the slim, soft growth at the tip. Make the cutting about 30cm (12in) long and trim just below a leaf joint at the base. Remove all lower leaves, but not the buds.

■ **Prepare a narrow,** V-shaped trench in the ground, about 23cm (9in) deep; half fill with sharp sand if the soil is heavy.

■ **Dip the base of the cuttings** in hormone rooting powder. Plant upright, 15cm (6in) apart, buried to half their length.

Dealing with rose suckers

1 Suckers are vigorous shoots that grow from below ground on grafted roses and also from the stems of standards. Trace them back to their origin, clearing away soil at the base of the rose to enable you to do this.

2 Wearing strong gardening gloves, tear off the sucker to prevent regrowth. Using secateurs would stimulate the rose to produce more suckers.

Pruning a rambler

1 Rambler roses will have finished flowering by the end of summer, and their growth will have become untidy and tangled. Untie all the stems from their supports, and select about six of the strongest, new green stems growing from the ground. These will be retained.

2 Prune out all the old, darker stems, cutting them close to ground level. If there is a shortage of new stems from ground level, cut back some of the older ones to a strong new shoot instead of cutting them right down.

3 Shorten all the fresh green sideshoots by at least two-thirds and ideally to leave only two to three buds, as shorter sideshoots will produce better regrowth next year. Once this is done, tie in the retained shoots to their supports, spreading them out evenly so the next season's flowers will be well distributed.

■ **Replace the soil** and tread it firm round the cuttings. Water well and label clearly. Check whether they have rooted in April but, preferably, leave until next autumn. It will take two years for cuttings to make substantial young plants, and perhaps a further season before they flower.

Preparing for new roses

Take the opportunity to visit rose gardens to see plants in bloom and read through some rose catalogues. Order plants in good time for autumn delivery.

Before then you need to prepare the site thoroughly. Make a start in late summer by digging the soil to around two spade blades deep. Remove weeds and root fragments and work in plenty of well-rotted manure or garden compost. Deep digging helps to improve drainage, but on very heavy ground it might be easier to create raised beds.

Lightly fork in a top-dressing of rose fertiliser and leave the soil to settle for at least six weeks.

TIP Avoid planting new roses where roses grew before as they are unlikely to thrive. If you have nowhere else to plant, you must replace the soil. Dig a hole for each new plant, about 60cm (2ft) wide and 45cm (18in) deep. Remove the excavated soil to elsewhere in the garden and replace it with a mixture of fresh topsoil and garden compost or well-rotted manure.

76 | Climbers

Climbers and wall shrubs grow rapidly now, and new shoots need tying in regularly. Pruning may be necessary to keep plants tidy and encourage more flowers. In late summer, take advantage of maturing growth to make semi-ripe cuttings and prepare the ground for planting new climbers in autumn.

Summer checklist

■ **Train and tie in climbers** regularly to produce an attractive display, otherwise many rapidly form a bird's nest of stems that it is impossible to unravel. Prime candidates for attention are those that climb by means of tendrils or twining leaf stalks, such as clematis, particularly *Clematis armandii*, and sweet peas (*Lathyrus odoratus*). Use soft string for tying in, not

wire. As growth slows later in the summer, attend to plants on a fortnightly, rather than a weekly, basis.

■ **Water container-grown climbers** daily unless rainfall is plentiful, as well as any that are newly planted. Add a liquid fertiliser to the water once a week, or add slow-release fertiliser to the compost.

■ **Check climbers trained** against buildings as they form another priority group. Even when the plants are established they may need watering if the structure against which they are growing shelters the soil, keeping off most of the rain. Give them a soaking every couple of weeks, increasing the frequency in drought periods.

■ **Prune spring-flowering clematis**, such as *C. alpina* and *C. macropetala*, if you have not already done so.

■ **Prune climbers that have already** flowered if next year's blooms are carried on stems produced this summer.

■ **Plant permanent climbers** and wall shrubs, but remember to water them regularly during dry spells until the autumn.

■ **Propagate climbers and wall shrubs** from semi-ripe cuttings (see page 79).

■ **Pot up rooted cuttings** taken in spring that are now well established.

■ **Watch out for clematis wilt.** This fungal disease causes part or all of the clematis to collapse suddenly. The young leaves and upper parts of shoots wilt first and the leaf stalks blacken where they meet the blade. You can help your plant to survive an attack by planting it 15cm (6in) deeper than it was in the pot (buds below ground

Clematis **Blue Moon, with its ruffled petals** and maroon anthers, produces an attractive display from late spring to early summer and then flowers again in early autumn.

Summer-pruning wisteria

1 Prune young wisteria shoots in midsummer as well as any long, whippy growths not required to make new branches. Leave five or six buds.

2 This tidies the overall shape of the wisteria, and then the winter prune will reduce sideshoots, leaving three buds on all growth that has appeared since the summer pruning. This pruning regime ensures a neat shape and plenty of flowers.

usually survive to shoot and provide replacement growth). Cut back any affected stems to healthy growth and then burn any diseased material – do not put it on the compost heap.

■ **Prune wisteria** as soon as possible if this task was not done earlier in summer.

■ **Control self-clinging climbers,** which can damage woodwork and guttering.

■ **Weed regularly** and watch out for bindweed in particular.

■ **Check leaf-bud cuttings of clematis** that were taken in late spring once new leaves begin to appear.

■ **Stay alert for signs of fungal diseases,** which are likely to be a problem if the weather has been extremely wet or dry.

An application of fungicide usually limits further spread of the disease but does not cure affected foliage, which should be cut off and removed or destroyed.

■ **Watch out for pests.** Aphids often infest annual climbers, and nasturtiums are especially susceptible to attack by the larvae of the cabbage white butterfly. Regular inspections are essential, and removing caterpillars by hand is usually enough to keep populations in check.

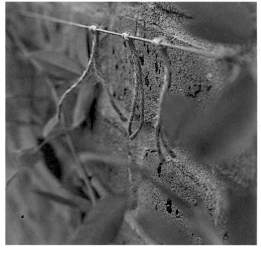

Attach string ties to wire supports before climbers put on a spurt of growth in summer; this makes it easier to tie the plants in when they reach the wire.

■ **Feed annual climbers** every seven to 14 days with liquid fertiliser to keep them flowering. Do not feed permanent plants, however, as this encourages soft growth that could be damaged later by frost.

■ **Prepare ground for autumn planting** of hardy climbers. Dig the soil to two spade blades deep and incorporate plenty of well-rotted organic matter.

Pruning

Many climbers and wall shrubs need pruning now to keep them within bounds and to encourage prolific flowering.

Clematis montana and its cultivars

Cut these back to keep them within their allotted space. Shorten stems as soon as possible after flowering because next year's blooms are carried on growth that is produced this summer.

■ **To avoid having to prune** these rampant climbers, plant the compact cultivar 'Primrose Star', which grows to a height of only 3m (10ft).

Early flowering honeysuckles

Prune honeysuckles, such as the early *Lonicera periclymenum* and its cultivars, immediately after flowering.

■ **Cut back the stems that flowered** to strong, young growth in order to keep the plant neat and bushy.

Firethorn and flowering quince

Train *Pyracantha* and *Chaenomeles* close to their supports. Prune them, and other wall-trained shrubs, immediately after flowering.

■ **Cut back all outward-facing shoots** to two or three buds and tie in the others.

Wisteria

Prune wisteria twice a year, in midsummer (see page 77) and again in winter. Tie in new stems left unpruned and train them horizontally if possible, which will boost flowering by slowing the flow of sap along the branches.

Summer-flowering climbers

These benefit from being pruned back by one-third immediately after flowering. These include akebia, escallonia, summer jasmine and passion flower.

■ **Count the number of main shoots** at or just above ground level, from which the sideshoots grow. Decide how many main shoots must be removed to achieve the target of one-third.

■ **Cut the selected shoots one at a time** as near the base as possible then leave them *in situ* overnight. The foliage on the cut shoots will wilt making it easier to identify them.

■ **Cut out the wilted shoots in sections:** don't try to pull them out complete or you will damage the plant.

Overgrown climbers

Prune other climbers if they extend beyond their allotted space, but remember that by pruning flowering climbers in late summer you are likely to be removing next year's blooms.

Pruning and training climbers

1 Main stems should be spaced out evenly and at an angle from the vertical. Next, secure them to their support using soft twine tied in a figure of eight.

2 Wayward stems should be trimmed back to just above a leaf joint. This will need to be done regularly for vigorous climbers.

The leaves of *Parthenocissus henryana* turn a striking red in autumn, but ensure its sucker pads are kept away from paintwork.

Self-clinging climbers Keep climbers like ivy, virginia creepers and *Parthenocissus henryana* clear of window frames and other woodwork, as their clinging stem roots or sucker pads are likely to cause damage, particularly to paintwork.

■ **Trim back growth** to at least 30cm (12in) from susceptible areas of the house. Train or prune the stems to keep them clear of roof edges, guttering and downpipes.

Propagation

Many climbers can be raised now from semi-ripe cuttings. The chief exception is clematis, which are best propagated by internodal leaf-bud cuttings (see page 33). If you took any of these earlier in the year, check them once new leaves begin to appear by carefully taking off the pot. If roots are developing, pot up the cuttings individually into 8cm (3in) pots.

Semi-ripe cuttings Select healthy, non-flowering shoots when the stem is firm but not yet hard and woody. Sever them from the parent plant just above a leaf joint.

■ **Make the cuttings** about 10–15cm (4–6in) long by trimming just below a leaf joint, using a sharp knife. Remove the leaves on the lower two-thirds of the shoot.

■ **Dip the base of each cutting** in hormone rooting compound, then insert several cuttings around the edge of a 13cm (5in) pot filled with moist cuttings and seed compost. Rooting is improved if the compost is mixed with a third by volume of perlite or horticultural vermiculite.

■ **Stand the pot of cuttings** in a propagator or coldframe shaded from the sun. Do not over-water, but do not let them dry out completely. Rooting usually takes between eight and 12 weeks.

Controlling bindweed

Weeds often grow unnoticed through established climbers, and bindweed is a particular nuisance as it twines up their stems. Midsummer is a good time to apply the systemic weedkiller glyphosate to this and other tenacious perennial weeds, before they flower and set seed. Because the chemical kills any growth it touches, start by training the bindweed away from the host climber by sticking bamboo canes into the ground up which the weed can grow. Then slip the growth off the canes and apply the glyphosate within a polythene bag, to prevent it from coming into contact with other plants.

Bindweed, a strong-growing twining weed, can strangle other plants if not removed quickly using a glyphosate weedkiller.

80 Shrubs and trees

Covered in bright, fresh foliage and with many in full flower, the challenge this season is to keep shrubs and trees in peak condition. Maintain a regular routine of watering, weeding, pruning, hedge trimming and pest control. This is also the perfect time to propagate a wide variety of shrubs.

Summer checklist

■ **Trim fast-growing hedges** such as privet and lonicera regularly to keep them looking immaculate.

■ **Remove the fleece** from cold-sensitive shrubs that needed protection from frost at night, now that temperatures are rising.

■ **Move outdoors any tender shrubs** in containers, such as citrus or oleander (*Nerium*), that were kept under glass during winter. Give them a sunny, sheltered spot.

■ **Water and feed during dry weather.** Concentrate on freshly planted and container shrubs and trees.

■ **Eradicate weeds** by hoeing and hand-weeding, digging them up before they have a chance to establish. Pay special attention to the areas around new plants and hedges.

Look under spreading branches in case perennial weeds such as dock are growing and shedding seeds unnoticed; the old adage 'one year's seeding means seven years weeding' is true.

■ **Support and tie in the new growth** of plants being trained against a wall or trellis.

■ **Inspect plants for signs of pests or diseases.**

Buddleja is just one of many flowering shrubs at their best during summer. The deep purple blooms of *Buddleja davidii* 'Black Knight' will attract butterflies to the garden.

These are more likely to be a problem if shrubs have been under stress due to drought or if the weather has been unduly wet. Established shrubs usually shrug off all but severe attacks but it is worth checking young plants and those growing in containers, and controlling any attacks detected in the early stages before they do serious damage.

■ **Prune shrubs** such as broom (*Cytisus*) and flowering quince (*Chaenomeles)* as soon as they finish flowering, removing a third of overgrown leafy plants (see opposite).

■ **Prune ornamental plums,** cherries and almonds to ensure they stay in perfect shape once they are in full leaf. If you do it when they are dormant they are more susceptible to disease.

■ **Spur prune wall-trained** *Chaenomeles* and *Pyracantha* in July (see page 82). This thins out any congested tangles of spurs – the clusters of mini branches off the main branches – where the flowers grow.

■ **Remove the flowers** from grey-leaved shrubs, like senecio or helichrysum, grown for their foliage or as formal hedges.

■ **Thin out the crowns** of congested broad-leaved trees such as crab apples (*Malus*) and acers that heavily shade plants beneath them (see page 83).

■ **Pot up or transplant seedlings** from earlier sowings, giving them more space to continue developing.

■ **Pot up rooted soft-tip cuttings,** and take more if required using the young sideshoots on established plants.

■ **Start taking semi-ripe cuttings** from conifers using the mid or late summer growth (see page 85).

■ **Move camellias in containers** out of bright sunshine into partial shade.

■ **Continue layering plants** such as the smoke bush (*Cotinus*) and magnolias (see page 39).

■ **Feed hardy fuchsias** once or twice with a high-potash fertiliser to encourage prolific flowering all summer.

■ **Protect exposed hydrangeas** from hot, dry winds with a screen of net curtaining or a similar fine material, otherwise they may suffer from scorching.

■ **Start deadheading lilac** (*Syringa*) and later flowering rhododendrons before new shoots begin developing behind the withered flowers.

■ **Trim hedges to keep them neat,** giving formal hedges their final trim in late summer (see page 87).

■ **Check variegated shrubs** and remove any single-coloured shoots.

■ **Prune early-flowering shrubs** as soon as their flowers fade.

■ **Keep camellias moist** as they can suffer from bud drop and, consequently, loss of flowers in the coming spring due to a shortage of water now. Take care not to let the plants dry out, and cover the soil with a 5cm (2in) layer of mulch to help maintain moisture in the soil.

The one-third prune

1 Prune away a third of a leafy overgrown shrub as soon as the flowers have died down.

2 Weak, spindly shoots and stems that cross or crowd each other out must be cut out using a pair of sharp secateurs.

3 Use a pruning saw to remove a number of the oldest branches just above ground level or to a low, strong sideshoot.

4 Aim to remove a third of the growth annually, so that no branch on the shrub is more than three years old. This will admit light to the shrub and maintain a good shape and strong growth.

Pruning

Cut out any green-leaved or reverted shoots – these occur commonly on shrubs with coloured or variegated foliage. Prune these out as soon as possible, because they grow fast and, if left, will eventually dominate the plant. Reversion is much less likely to occur on flowering shrubs, but tree mallow (*Lavatera*) may produce shoots with blooms of a different colour and you should prune these out too.

Trim lavender and cotton lavender (*Santolina chamaecyparissus*) after flowering to keep plants neat. You can do this by simply shearing off the flowerheads.

Shrubs and informal hedges that flower in May and early June, on stems produced the previous year, need to be pruned annually. This prevents twiggy growth and sparse blooms next year. It is best done immediately after flowering to allow plenty of time for new growth to develop and ripen before the end of the season. How hard you prune depends on the age, size and condition of the shrub.

Formative pruning For the first two to three years of a shrub's life, pruning helps form a strong framework of branches and a balanced shape.

■ **After planting, remove any damaged** or weak, spindly growth from the shrub, and lightly trim back the shoot tips to a strong bud, or pair of buds.

■ **In the autumn, cut out** any weak shoots and those that unbalance the overall shape.

■ **Repeat this formative pruning** for the next two years, also pruning in midsummer those shoots that carried flowers; cut them back to about 5cm (2in) long.

Renewal pruning This is the simplest way to maintain a compact shape and a vigorous supply of young, floriferous growth on shrubs that are over three years old. As a third of the growth is removed, it is often called the one-third prune (see page 81).

Spur pruning When trained on a wall, either growing freely or pruned as a fan or espalier, *Pyracantha* and *Chaenomeles* will need spur pruning. This maintains their shape and maximises flowering.

■ **About two weeks before** midsummer, remove all crossing or inward growing shoots and shorten those growing away from the wall, to leave four to six leaves. This encourages the formation of flowering shoots and, in the case of *Pyracantha*, exposes the colourful berries.

Shearing lavender

1 After any stems have been removed for drying and lavender bushes are coming to the end of their flowering cycle, clip them all over.

2 Use garden shears to take off the dead flowers complete with stems and the top few centimetres of any long new shoots.

finished, to about 10cm (4in) from their base. Where they meet older main branches, do not cut into these because the main branches do not readily produce new shoots.

■ **Tie any stems that are growing** sideways against the wall.

■ **Check again in early autumn** and shorten any excessively long new shoots.

Crown thinning A broad-leaved tree with a dense or cluttered canopy of branches may cast so much shade that little will grow beneath it. The technique of crown thinning is used to remove several branches, creating greater penetration of air and light, without altering the tree's size and shape.

Tall trees should be thinned by a qualified tree surgeon, but on a smaller tree you can do this yourself. Do the work in midsummer to assess how much the shade is reduced, and because re-growth will be less vigorous than after winter surgery. The following winter, check to see whether further light pruning is needed to improve the balance and symmetry of the bare branches.

■ **Start by cutting out dead,** damaged and diseased wood, followed by any branches that cross or rub against each other. Also cut out branches that grow across or into the centre of the tree.

■ **Reduce pairs of branches** that form narrow angles to a single, strong branch. If necessary, trim back any low branches that are creating an obstruction at head height, and any that are too long, unbalanced or too close to other branches.

■ **Aim to remove no more** than a third of the healthy branches.

Propagation

Close to midsummer, the garden will be full of young growth that can be used as cuttings, creating new plants by autumn or the following spring. You can take several kinds of cuttings, while many shrubs can be layered where they grow by pegging branches down in the soil (see page 39).

Ceanothus '**Italian Skies**' is best grown against a wall, where it will produce showy clusters of blue flowers.

■ **In early autumn,** further shorten the pruned shoots, leaving just two to three leaves on each.

Pruning broom If broom (*Cytisus*) is left unpruned it soon becomes top-heavy and short-lived. It is best to prune young plants in early summer.

■ **Pinch out the growing tips** of young plants to keep them bushy and cut back the current year's growth by half immediately after flowering to control the shrub's size. Never prune into woody growth as this can kill the plant.

Pruning evergreen ceanothus

Evergreen varieties are often injured by frosts unless they are grown against a sunny, sheltered wall, where they need regular pruning to maintain their shape and vigour. The majority bloom in spring or early summer, and should be pruned immediately the flowers have faded.

■ **Trim back the shoots** growing away from the wall, on which the flowers have just

Soft-tip cuttings These are the soft tips taken from main stems and sideshoots. They may be rooted in covered pots or trays, in the greenhouse or on a windowsill out of direct sunlight (see page 39).

Semi-ripe cuttings The sideshoots on shrubs that started growing early in the season are forming woody tissue at their base by midsummer. You can feel this as a slight firmness when you gently bend a shoot with your fingers. Cuttings from these shoots take a little longer to root than soft cuttings, but are less likely to dry out or to rot if conditions are too wet.

Choose healthy, non-flowering shoots that are starting to turn woody. Sever them from the parent plant by cutting just above a leaf joint to avoid leaving a stump of dead stem. In some cases you can take cuttings with a 'heel', a strip of older wood at the base of the shoot. These have an even better chance of success because the plant's growth hormones that stimulate rooting are concentrated in the heel.

Semi-ripe cuttings are normally prepared with the aid of rooting hormone powder or liquid, and can be grown in containers filled with cuttings compost. After inserting the cuttings in a pot, water and cover it with an inflated clear polythene bag, or stand it in a propagator or coldframe, out of direct sun, and leave. Rooting usually takes six to ten weeks, but longer in the case of evergreens.

Semi-ripe cuttings can also be grown in the ground under a cloche or in a coldframe. Choose a warm, sunny or lightly shaded position. A sheet of bubble polythene makes an excellent cloche cover. Alternatively, coat glass cloches and glazed coldframes with a thin speckling of greenhouse shade paint.

■ **Fork over the soil** where the cuttings are to go. Remove all weeds and stones, rake level and cover the surface with a

In summer, semi-ripe cuttings can be taken from shrubs such as senecio, euonymus, yew and box; choose healthy, non-flowering shoots.

Taking semi-ripe cuttings

1 Gently pull off 10cm (4in) long sideshoots. This will leave a 'heel' of tissue at the base. Trim the heel with a sharp knife to give a clean edge, and remove all except the top five to ten leaves. Dip the base of the cuttings in hormone rooting powder, and shake off any surplus.

2 Use a dibber or plant label to make holes in the soil or cuttings compost. Insert the cuttings to a depth of 5cm (2in) and position them 5cm (2in) apart, in rows in the ground or round the rim of a 13cm (5in) pot; firm in.

3 Choose a warm, sunny position, water in well and cover with a cloche or the lid of a coldframe or propagator. Keep closed, but check weekly to see that the soil is not drying out. Rooting takes six to ten weeks.

2–3cm (1in) layer of grit and perlite, in equal parts. Mix this into the top 5cm (2in) of soil with a hand fork. Prepare and plant the cuttings (see above), then cover them with a cloche or close the coldframe.

■ **Check after four to six weeks** to see if there is rooting and new growth. If there is, raise the lid or side of the cloche a little to let in some air. Keep the cuttings moist by watering, and mist occasionally with a spray in hot weather. Rooted cuttings that are growing vigorously may be moved to a 'nursery bed' or spare piece of ground in autumn, but it is generally safer to wait until next spring before replanting the cuttings 30cm (12in) apart. Plant the young plantlets out permanently the following autumn.

TIP When using rooting hormone never dip your cuttings into the main container: pour a little of the hormone into a dish, and discard any that is left over after use. Insert only the bottom tip of the cutting in the hormone, shaking or tapping off any surplus. Keep rooting powder or liquid in the fridge for prolonged life – clearly labelled – and replace annually with a fresh supply.

Azalea cuttings Some lime-hating plants – such as japanese azaleas, enkianthus, gaultheria, kalmia, vaccinium and pieris – need slightly different treatment.

■ **Take cuttings of 5cm (2in) sideshoots** and root in a coldframe or gently heated propagator in a greenhouse. Prepare them as for other semi-ripe cuttings (see above) and insert them 1cm (½in) deep in small pots filled with a mixture of equal parts lime-free grit and perlite.

■ **Water well and keep** shut in a coldframe or lidded propagator until late autumn. Then transfer to a cool bench in the greenhouse.

■ **Feed with a high-potash** liquid fertiliser in early spring. When new shoots appear in early summer, pot them up individually in lime-free compost.

Conifer cuttings Take semi-ripe cuttings, 5–8cm (2–3in) long, each with a 'heel'. Nip off sideshoots from the lower half of the cutting and carefully trim the bark away from one side of the lower 2–3cm (1in) with a sharp knife.

Conifers are easily raised from semi-ripe cuttings; these recycled cans make perfect pots for use in a greenhouse or propagator.

■ **Root them with the aid** of hormone powder and plant 1cm (½in) deep in small pots filled with equal parts grit and perlite.

■ **Keep the cuttings covered** in a propagator or with a clear plastic bag, and stand them in a warm but shady part of the greenhouse or on a windowsill. New growth should be visible by mid-autumn. If they fail to root, take a further batch of cuttings.

Leaf-bud cuttings An economical method of propagating evergreen shrubs where you want several cuttings from one shoot, or if there is not enough suitable material on the parent plant (such as after a poor summer, producing little growth).

■ **Select semi-ripe shoots** as described above, but cut each one into sections, 2–3cm (1in) below a leaf joint and immediately above the leaf.

■ **Remove a sliver of bark** from the stem below the leaf joint to stimulate rooting.

■ **Insert the cuttings into a pot** or tray filled with cuttings compost so that the top of the leaf joint is just visible above the surface of the compost. Then treat as described under semi-ripe cuttings.

Watering

Check shrubs, trees and hedges planted earlier in the year regularly, and water if necessary, especially during prolonged dry or windy weather.

■ **When watering, thoroughly soak** the ground right round the base of the plant, ideally following with a thick mulch to 'lock' the moisture in the soil. Water early in the morning or late afternoon to avoid the risk of scorching on splashed leaves.

■ **Add a liquid fertiliser** at the recommended rate when watering new plants, and any that have been hard-pruned or which show signs of poor growth. Apply a foliar feed to the leaves after sunset to give a quick tonic to ailing plants.

■ **Check plants in containers** daily and move to a sheltered, lightly shaded position if they dry out rapidly; a mulch of pebbles or gravel helps to prevent moisture loss.

Weeding

Continue to eradicate weeds by hoeing and hand-weeding. This applies particularly to the immediate area around new shrubs, trees and hedges, as they need a couple of seasons without any competition. Keep at least 1m² (1sq yd) around the base of the plant weed-free by hoeing, spraying or laying a woven mulching mat.

If you plan to make a new bed or border this autumn, it is best to clear the site now and spray it with glyphosate, or a similar chemical, to kill perennial weeds. This gives surviving roots and weed seeds time to regenerate and be forked out before planting. The traditional method for getting rid of weed roots is to dig the area thoroughly, removing by hand every trace of weeds, including root fragments.

Trimming hedges

Late summer is the time to give formal hedges their final trim for the year, as pruning in autumn encourages soft new growth that could be damaged by frost. Some informal hedges also benefit from attention now, notably those that have finished flowering.

Established formal hedges require regular trimming along the top and sides to maintain a neat shape, whereas informal hedges, mostly grown for their flowers or berries, should be left to grow more naturally. A neat formal hedge will need to be cut between one and three times during the growing season; the frequency depends on how quickly your chosen plant grows.

Start trimming as soon as a recently planted hedge reaches the required height (for conifers, see below). If allowed to get out of hand, the hedge may not regrow if pruned hard later on. By beginning regular trimming at an early stage, even the most rampant of hedge plants can be kept compact. Shape the hedge so that the top is narrower than the bottom. This makes it less vulnerable to wind and snow.

Hedge-trimming tools

The choice of equipment depends on the size of hedge and the amount of energy you have. Garden shears for hand trimming come in lightweight and heavy-duty models. Choose light ones for a soft-stemmed hedge,

Trimming a formal conifer hedge

1 Before cutting conifers, allow the hedge to grow about 60cm (2ft) above the desired height. Run a string between two canes at the cutting height, which will be around 15cm (6in) below the ultimate level. This will encourage new bushy growth at the top.

2 Trim the sides, starting at the bottom and working upwards, and making the hedge narrower at the top than it is at the base. Wear goggles and gloves when using a powered hedge trimmer and, if electric, always use a circuit breaker, or RCD, for safety.

3 Using your string guideline, cut the top of the hedge, tapering the edges rather than leaving a flat, wide top. Do not overreach; if necessary, set up a ladder or trestles and make sure they stand on a firm, level base. Get a helper to steady the bottom of a ladder while you are working.

Hedge trimming times

FORMAL HEDGES	WHEN TO TRIM
Box* (*Buxus sempervirens*)	Once, late summer
Hornbeam* (*Carpinus betulus*)	Once, mid to late summer
Lawson's cypress (*Chamaecyparis lawsoniana*)	Twice, spring and autumn
Hawthorn* (*Crataegus monogyna*)	Twice, summer and winter
Leyland cypress (x *Cupressocyparis leylandii*)	2–3 times in growing season
Beech* (*Fagus sylvatica*)	Once, late summer
Holly* (*Ilex aquifolium*)	Once, late summer
Privet* (*Ligustrum ovalifolium*)	2–3 times in growing season
Laurel* (*Prunus laurocerasus*)	Once, spring
Yew* (*Taxus baccata*)	Twice, summer and autumn

INFORMAL HEDGES	WHEN TO TRIM
Berberis species and cultivars*	Immediately after flowering
Elaeagnus species and cultivars	In spring, removing straggly shoots only
Escallonia species and cultivars*	Late summer
Griselinia littoralis	In spring, removing straggly shoots only
Lavender (*Lavandula angustifolia*)	Lightly in spring and again after flowering to remove dead flower stems and tips of new shoots
Pyracantha species and cultivars	Summer
Rosa rugosa	Remove thin shoots in spring
Viburnum tinus	Thin out growth in spring

* plants that tolerate hard pruning and renovation

but use a heavier model for thicker growth. Shears with telescopic handles give extra long reach for tall hedges.

Hedge trimmers come in a range of sizes and are powered by petrol or electricity. For safety, use a circuit breaker, or residual current device (RCD), when operating an electric hedge trimmer from the mains. Wear protective clothing and do not work in wet conditions. Rechargeable battery-powered trimmers are safer.

TIP Prune large-leaved evergreen hedging plants, such as common laurel, with secateurs to avoid shearing leaves in half and leaving their unsightly browning remains.

Overgrown hedges

Neglected and overgrown hedges can often be given a new lease of life by hard pruning. This helps to ensure that they remain dense and continue as an effective barrier. However, some plants do not respond well to hard pruning, as they do not produce new growth on old wood. This includes, most notably, the leyland and lawson's cypresses. Such plants are best cut down, dug up and replaced if they have become at all thin or bare at the base.

It's best to leave the hard pruning of evergreens to mid-spring. Renovate deciduous hedges in winter.

Now is the time to enjoy your patio. Rearrange the containers to create different colour combinations, give scented plants a prominent position and save some space for last-minute purchases. Keep plants fresh by watering and deadheading regularly, and take soft-tip cuttings of any favourite flowers.

Summer checklist

■ **Hang up baskets** and stand out pots of tender bedding, but make sure they have been hardened off first.

■ **Water all plants** growing in containers, and mulch raised beds to conserve moisture (see page 92). Plants in containers should be watered until you see the surplus running out through the drainage holes, as it is possible for large containers to dry out completely without you realising.

■ **Keep deadheading** for prolonged flowering (see page 90) and remove faded leaves and straggly stems.

■ **Regularly feed plants** in hanging baskets and other containers to ensure optimum performance (see page 90).

■ **Give all plants a regular check,** even if it means getting down on your hands and knees to make sure they really are healthy. Look under the leaves where aphids might be lurking, and examine the stems closely.

■ **Check under large planters** from time to time to see that ants are not marching in through the drainage holes and creating nests in the compost.

■ **Group together pots and tubs** of flowering plants, to create eye-catching combinations on the patio.

■ **Put scented plants** in a sheltered, sunny position by seating areas or near open windows for maximum benefit.

■ **Remove a paving slab** on the patio, dig down a spade's depth, add topsoil, compost and horticultural sand, and plant scented herbs, such as thyme (see page 91).

■ **Leave room for impulse buys** to jazz up a raised bed or a container grouping. Look out for unusual or tender plants at the garden centre to enhance your display.

■ **When buying tender plants** bear in mind that conditions on your patio might be cooler or windier than the protected environment at the garden centre where the plant has been growing, so gradually acclimatise it to your garden.

■ **Feed flagging plants,** as the growth rate slows down in late summer. An extra boost of tomato feed should rejuvenate them and help them to continue flowering until the first frost.

■ **Trim overgrown topiary** so it retains its shape until next summer (see page 91).

■ **Take soft-tip cuttings** of tender plants you would like to use again next year.

■ **Weed the cracks between paving** before the weeds get too established and have a chance to set seed.

■ **Plant up a container or two** in late summer for autumn and winter beauty.

This eye-catching window box blends fuchsias, pelargoniums, mimulas and nasturtiums. Remove and replace plants as they fade to ensure floral continuity all summer.

Feeding container plants

Regular summer feeding is essential for plants growing in containers or they will develop pale leaves and perform badly.

■ **If you have not added** a slow-release fertiliser at planting time, start feeding now, every seven to 14 days. Use a high-nitrogen fertiliser for newly planted baskets and containers. Swap to a tomato feed after three weeks, to encourage flowering until autumn. Do not exceed the manufacturer's recommended dose; a high concentration of chemicals will do more harm than good.

■ **Use a liquid feed** or slow-release fertiliser sticks or capsules.

Deadheading

Promptly snipping off fading or dead flowers does two things: it gets rid of insipid colours that detract from the overall display, and it ensures that plants channel their energy into creating more beautiful flowers instead of developing the seed heads.

■ **Deadhead patio roses** quite severely after blooming, removing entire flower sprays.

■ **Radically cut back violas,** most geraniums, campanulas and convolvulus to promote a second flush of bloom.

TIP After cutting the growth back, give the plants a thorough watering and a light application of plant food, such as a dilute liquid feed. This will stimulate new growth and plenty of flowers.

Holiday survival guide

This is the traditional season for getting away from the garden, but before you depart make provision for your patio plants so that they survive your absence.

■ **Arrange for a neighbour** to come in and water your containers, or consider installing an automatic watering system (see page 92).

■ **Group containers together** in one spot, which is both out of the sun and sheltered from the wind. Not only does this make watering more convenient for your neighbour, it also means pots are less likely to dry out if left unattended for a day or two.

■ **Plunge small pots into** a bigger container filled with moist sand or potting compost.

■ **Incorporate water-retaining** gel into the compost of thirsty summer bedding when planting or repotting. The gel mops up excess moisture, preventing waterlogging, but roots are still able to extract the water when they need it.

■ **Cut off surplus growth,** as plants pruned quite hard will need watering less frequently than those with an excessive amount of

---

Propagating tender perennials

This is the time to take cuttings of tender perennials, so attractive during summer but costly to buy. Taking soft-tip cuttings will ensure that you have plentiful stocks of mature plants, ready to set out in beds and containers in late spring next year. Ideally, select non-flowering shoots. If this is not possible, remove the flowers before making and inserting the cuttings in a tray or round the edge of a container (see page 61).

If you plan to grow lots of cuttings, you will need a greenhouse or a well-lit conservatory. But even if you lack these facilities and space is limited, it should still be possible to overwinter a few of your favourites for next year on a windowsill indoors.

When potting up rooted cuttings, avoid using containers that are too large. The compost could become wet and stagnant, and the young roots rot off. It is better to pot them now into small containers and pot them on later, in February, when the days are lengthening and growth begins in earnest.

leaves and stems. Feed and water plants thoroughly immediately after pruning, to initiate healthy re-growth.

■ **Pick off flowers and buds,** if these are likely to open while you are away. Removing young flower spikes from such plants as penstemons, phygelius, nemesias and diascias should stimulate a burst of fresh growth to greet your return.

Trimming topiary

This is the best time for trimming topiary in pots, as there is still enough growing season left for it to recover from being shorn, but not enough to grow untidy. In this way specimens will retain their neat shape until next summer. The number of trims per year depends on the plant (see Hedge Trimming Times chart, page 88).

Trimming by eye is usually sufficient for simple shapes, although you can use a wooden frame as a guide. More intricate designs are probably best trained on a wire-netting frame, which makes them easier to trim to shape. Shears or mechanical hedge clippers are suitable for topiary work, although shrubs with large, evergreen leaves, like laurel, may look unsightly unless trimmed with secateurs. Shears cut across leaves, which stain and distort as they heal.

It is easier to trim topiary shrubs in containers than those in borders, which can grow very large. Keep the topiary form in harmony with the container's shape and in proportion to its size.

Planting thyme

Add interest to your patio by planting a few thymes in full sun between the paving. The plants' essential oils will be released when trod upon.

■ Lift a paving slab and dig out the soil to a spade's depth. Replace it with a mix of topsoil, compost and horticultural sand for good drainage.

■ Plant spreading, creeping thymes, such as *Thymus serpyllum* – these can also be planted in the cracks between the paving. Alternatively, plant taller species, like *T. vulgaris*, that can be pruned to give a rounded shape.

Keeping topiary in trim

1 Use lightweight garden shears to trim small-leaved topiary in pots, such as box. Trimming now will help define the shape better and neaten the plant.
2 Follow your eye and carefully snip away until you have achieved the desired shape and a good size for the pot.

WATERING POT PLANTS

Plants in pots have a limited root area from which to take up moisture, and the situation is compounded by an 'umbrella' of foliage that keeps most rainfall off the compost. Watering can become a time-consuming chore in summer, when plants can need attention once or even twice a day.

The frequency of watering can be reduced by using water-retaining gels, self-watering containers and large pots. Even better, cut the workload dramatically by installing a watering system; the addition of a timer will make the system completely automatic.

Choosing containers

The size and type of container, along with the amount of plant growth it has to support, influences how quickly the compost dries out. Hanging baskets dry out fastest, as the whole container is exposed to sun and wind. Pots made of porous material like terracotta also dry out quickly, though you can reduce water loss by lining the inside of the container (not the base) with polythene.

Large containers are best at retaining water as there is more compost to hold the moisture. Opt for generous containers and put a selection of plants in each one, rather than having lots of smaller pots.

Self-watering containers are a simple way to reduce the amount of watering required as they incorporate a built-in

An effective watering system involves running lengths of flexible microbore tubing between all your pots (left).
A drip nozzle is attached to the microbore tubing and delivers a fine spray of water to the base of plants in containers (below).

Constructing a watering system

1 Place your containers exactly where you want them on the patio. From the tap, run a length of rigid hose where it will be least obvious – along the base of a wall, for example. Measure the distance from your hosepipe to the first container, then measure the distances between the pots. This will give the number and lengths of tubing needed.

2 Using scissors or the tool provided with the kit, cut lengths of tubing. Fit a drip nozzle to the end of the first tube and peg it into a container before joining the next length of tubing up to it. Fix the other end of the first length of tubing to the hosepipe, using the attachment supplied.

3 Continue to fit tubes and drip nozzles to all containers. The easiest way to fit the tubes to the drip nozzles is to dip the ends of the tubing into a bowl of hot water – this makes the plastic more flexible.

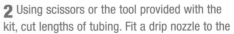

reservoir. The plant can take up water as necessary, but without the roots becoming waterlogged. This design is particularly useful for hanging baskets.

Patio watering systems

You can plumb your patio containers into a microbore watering system. A basic kit consists of a rigid hose running to the area to be watered. Flexible microbore tubing travels from the hose to the containers, delivering water to each pot by means of an attached drip nozzle (see above). The hose connects to a tap that you turn on manually, or you can fit a water timer (see right).

A watering system is perfect for containers as the water is delivered slowly and gently. Although fairly costly and time-consuming to set up, such a system can last for years, save time and keep your plants in good health.

Automatic watering

- **Make your watering system fully** automatic by fitting a timer. An automatic timer is designed to water once a day and is relatively inexpensive, while a computer-controlled timer gives much greater flexibility but costs almost twice as much.

- **Frequency and length of watering period** will vary, depending on site and weather conditions. Set up the timer at least a week before you go on holiday and monitor the amount of water required to keep the container compost evenly moist but not waterlogged. Set up the system during hot weather when the pipes will be more flexible.

- **In winter, make sure the system is** drained of water; this might freeze and cause damage. Dismantle and store under cover.

Now the weather is warmer, the lawn demands more of your time to keep it green and lush. Mowing is a dominant task, and regular cutting will keep your lawn looking smart. If the summer is dry, however, growth may be slow and the lawn will require a generous amount of watering.

Summer checklist

■ **Increase mowing** as the grass will be growing rapidly (see page 96). Maintain a regular mowing regime.

■ **Control lawn weeds** by raking or applying a weedkiller (see page 97).

■ **Clear moss early in the season** with an application of lawn sand containing sulphate of iron. In dry weather, water the lawn first so the lawn sand will stick to the moss. As it dies the moss will turn black then brown, at which stage you can rake it out using a fan-shaped rake. Burn or bin the dead moss; do not compost it.

■ **If moss reappears,** check the lawn to diagnose the problem. Moss in the lawn is usually a symptom of poor drainage (this will need to be improved by aerating and top dressing in autumn), heavy shade, an acid soil or of mowing too closely and leaving bare patches where moss will quickly re-establish. Killing the moss will only be a temporary measure, because if you fail to resolve the original source of the problem, the moss will always return.

■ **Trim edges every three to four weeks** immediately after mowing. Use a pair of long-handled shears or an electric edger to save bending and to cut close to the lawn edge, removing the untidy fringe of grass. Collect up the trimmings.

■ **Water the lawn in exceptionally dry** periods, particularly if the lawn is in its first season. The grasses in new lawns will not have developed the large root systems found in established turf and this makes them more vulnerable to drought. The best times to water are in the cool early morning or late evening, so that as much water soaks in as possible rather than being lost through evaporation (see page 97).

Pale patches appear if garden ornaments, children's toys or other objects are left on the lawn; move things regularly to prevent this.

■ **Feed the lawn regularly** to compensate for frequent mowing, which can starve the grass. In summer give an application of high-nitrogen fertiliser to keep the grass green, healthy and growing rapidly. Two days after mowing, and when the soil is moist, apply a granular feed and water it in (see page 48).

■ **Scarify the grass** if it feels soft and spongy to walk on; this is usually a sign that a layer of dead grass and clippings, or 'thatch', has formed. Use a fan-shaped rake in a vigorous combing action to clear off the dead material so that water and fertiliser can penetrate to the grass roots.

■ **At the end of summer, feed the lawn** with an autumn fertiliser containing phosphates and potash to help harden plant growth for autumn and winter. Apply two days after mowing, and be prepared to water the fertiliser in if it does not rain within two days.

■ **Examine your lawn** for signs of fungal disease like red thread, which will appear as bleached patches of grass, with leaves developing a pinkish tinge (see page 96).

Mowing frequency

How often you need to mow will vary according to how wet or dry the season is and the type of lawn you have. The points to remember, before following the guidelines given here, are never to reduce the height of the grass by more than a third at a single cut, and always to allow it to recover for a couple of days before cutting again.

■ **Fine ornamental lawns** need cutting as often as two or three times a week, to a height of about 6mm (¼in). Regular close mowing keeps out the coarser grass and weeds that could smother fine grasses.

■ **Cut average-use lawns** once or twice a week to approximately 1cm (½in).

■ **Hardwearing lawns,** designed for play, need one cut a week to about 2cm (¾in).

■ **For new lawns, leave the grass** slightly longer to reduce stress in dry weather. If you have a mower with a roller, alternate between mowing the grass and rolling it lightly. The rolling will bend over the grass shoots, encouraging them to form more leaves and shade for the roots.

■ **Avoid mowing too closely,** as this can reduce the vigour of the grass plants and make them more susceptible to attack from fungal diseases.

■ **Infrequent or erratic mowing** encourages moss and weeds to invade the lawn as it struggles to recover.

Average-use lawns should be mown regularly once or twice a week, depending on the weather conditions.

■ **Change direction each time** you mow to prevent the mower from forming ruts and ridges in the lawn. This will also make it easier for you to mow off taller weeds and any grass flower stalks.

■ **In dry conditions,** let the grass grow longer and raise your mower blade to a slightly higher setting: 2–3cm (1in) for fine lawns. The extra length will shade grass roots and reduce stress due to water loss.

■ **During long, dry periods** mow less frequently – about once every seven to ten days should suffice. By leaving a greater leaf area on each plant you reduce the pressure on it to produce more growth to feed itself.

Protecting lawn edges

By late summer, herbaceous plants will be flopping over the edges of borders unless you have put supports in place. This will cause the edges of the lawn to turn brown as well as making them difficult to mow. Insert either purpose-made support frames or twiggy 'pea sticks' to pull plants back, or use canes and string to keep leafy plants off the lawn (see right). The alternative is to lay a hard 'mowing edge', such as a row of bricks or a narrow path, between the edge of the lawn and any border.

Red thread disease

This disease can appear as bleached patches of grass, with the leaves taking on a pinkish tinge as summer progresses. The incidence of red thread disease is more common on fine-leaved lawns and those that are underfed, and where soils are sandy as the fertilisers are easily washed through.

■ **Feed the grass regularly** (with a high-nitrogen fertiliser in spring and early summer and a high-phosphate plus potash feed in late summer and autumn) and your lawn will gradually recover, although it may look unsightly for some time.

■ **Avoid cutting the grass too closely** as this will lead to stress, which in turn makes the lawn more vulnerable to fungal diseases.

A home-made support using bamboo canes and hazel twigs stops tall perennials from flopping onto the lawn, where they can cause the edges of the grass to turn brown.

Weeding

The best way to eradicate spreading weeds, especially over a large area, is to make regular applications of lawn weedkiller during summer, in conjunction with frequent mowing. Remember that plants 'drink', rather than 'eat', so any product not already diluted must be accompanied by sufficient liquid to enable it to be taken up through the roots. For this reason, water your lawn thoroughly after each application of weedkiller if no heavy rain has fallen within two to three days. It is also worth pursuing the following strategies.

■ **Before mowing, rake the grass** well to lift weeds like speedwell and yarrow. This enables the cutting blade of the mower to slice off their top growth.

■ **Dig out perennial tap-rooted** weeds, such as dandelions, with an old knife or a special tool known as a grubber, to a depth of at least 7–8cm (3in) below soil level. Alternatively, spot-treat such weeds with a herbicide stick.

Watering

Turf can lose about 2–3cm (1in) of water every square metre over a period of one week during hot summer weather. To replace this you will need to apply about 25 litres (4 gallons) of water for every square metre of lawn. Using a lawn sprinkler is inexact in delivering water and can be wasteful in view of the volume that is lost to evaporation.

A more effective method is to place a seep or soaker hose on the lawn, connected to a tap, and leave it oozing water for at least half an hour (an hour in dry weather). Then move it to another site 1m (3ft) away and repeat the process. This allows water to penetrate the soil to a good depth, encouraging the grass to root down. If you can, water in the evening to minimise what is lost through evaporation.

TIP Applying a soluble fertiliser through an 'in-hose' dilutor saves you having to water the lawn after it has been fed as the dilutor combines the two operations.

A garden sprinkler is an inefficient method of watering the lawn as it delivers inexact amounts and a large volume of the water delivered is lost to evaporation.

98 The greenhouse

By now, many plants will have been moved outdoors. However, greenhouse crops and flowers will be at their peak and needing daily attention. With propagators and coldframes filling up with seedlings and cuttings, it is time to plan ahead. Sow annuals, force bulbs and give the greenhouse a good clean.

Summer checklist

■ **Take leaf cuttings** of gloxinias and African violets (*Saintpaulia*) (see page 100) and *Begonia rex* (see page 100). Take soft-tip cuttings of busy lizzies, houseplant ivies and tuberous begonias (see page 61).

■ **Take semi-ripe cuttings** of climbers and shrubs (see page 85). Propagate sturdy sideshoots of hydrangeas to root in individual 8cm (3in) pots, making flowering container plants for next year.

■ **Sow large-flowering cyclamen** to bloom in 18 months, and gently start watering last year's corms after their dormant period.

■ **Sow winter-flowering pansies,** primroses and polyanthus in trays in early June. Keep them in a shady part of the greenhouse or in a coldframe, and prick out into small pots when large enough.

You can raise alpines in the greenhouse. Plant in pots of gritty, open alpine compost and plunge in beds of grit or sharp sand.

■ **Sow tender perennials** such as gloxinias, tuberous begonias and streptocarpus in early June, and pot up seedlings to make sturdy young plants for keeping over winter.

■ **Prick out seedlings of cinerarias** (*Pericallis* x *hybrida*), calceolarias and other greenhouse flowers sown in late spring. Transfer them to individual cell-trays or 6cm (2½in) pots. When they fill their containers, move to larger pots and stand in a shady place outdoors.

■ **Pot up soft cuttings** started in May (see page 39) when new growth indicates successful rooting. Transfer them individually to 8cm (3in) pots, and keep lightly shaded for the first few days.

■ **Cut back regal pelargoniums** in July after flowering, and reduce watering to allow plants to rest.

■ **Check plants daily** to see if they require watering, more often in hot weather, or use an automatic system (see page 93). Also feed pot plants regularly, starting about six weeks after potting.

■ **Temperatures can soar under glass,** so it is important to keep them stable through a combination of shading, ventilation and damping down (see page 101).

■ **Inspect plants regularly** for the first signs of pests and diseases, and use biological controls as necessary (see page 103). Red spider mite is most likely to appear during August and can be controlled by the *Photoseiulus* parasite.

■ **Move greenhouse shrubs,** such as azaleas and camellias, outdoors. Stand or plunge their containers in deep sand or leaves, ideally in a coldframe, to keep them cool and moist (see page 103). Christmas cacti (*Schlumbergera*) can spend the summer outdoors in light shade.

You can help keep down pests in the greenhouse by suspending a piece of sticky card in a central spot. This will catch flying insects such as whitefly.

■ **Clean and store away** all greenhouse heating equipment now that the weather is hot and it is no longer needed.

■ **Pot up leftover bedding plants** for indoor colour. Ageratum, coleus, dwarf asters, *Begonia semperflorens* and heliotrope all make attractive windowsill plants in 13cm (5in) pots.

■ **Clean out an empty coldframe** and use it as an area for propagating new plants (see page 103).

■ **Scrub out pots** as they are emptied when the plants are put out. Before re-use, rinse them in a sterilising solution.

■ **Remove any dead flowers** and leaves, to keep them tidy and discourage disease.

■ **Keep the doors and windows** of your greenhouse open at all times during the summer if you are raising alpines; these plants need cool conditions with plenty of ventilation to prevent a build up of humidity. Also, increase the shading of any alpines growing under glass as temperatures rise.

■ **Prepare for your holiday,** especially if you have to leave plants unattended. Make sure they have been fed and make provisions for watering. Ensure that there is adequate shading to prevent overheating.

■ **Pot up rooted cuttings** you have taken of houseplants and shrubs.

■ **Prick out and pot on** flowering houseplants such as calceolarias and tender perennials as soon as they need more space. Feed them regularly, and stand in a cool, well-lit place.

■ **Gradually cease watering amaryllis** (*Hippeastrum*), which have now reached the end of their summer growth period, and allow the foliage to die down.

■ **Thoroughly clean and disinfect** inside the greenhouse in early September ready for next season's plants (see page 103).

■ **Bring indoors all pot plants** that have passed the summer outside, before the nights turn cold.

■ **Take semi-ripe cuttings** of your favourite shrubs, alpines and herbs (see page 85).

■ **Sow annuals for flowering under glass** during winter and spring, and annual herbs for winter use.

■ **Plant bulbs in pots for indoor display** over the winter (see page 101).

■ **Pot up arum lilies** after their summer rest (see page 100).

■ **Collect lily bulbils** and plant in trays.

■ **Encourage poinsettias** and Christmas cacti to flower at Christmas (see page 101).

■ **Plant *Anemone coronaria*** at the end of summer for flowers from late winter on. Space tubers 10–15cm (4–6in) apart and 8cm (3in) deep in a coldframe or a greenhouse border.

■ **Sow spring-flowering cinerarias** and indoor primroses, such as *Primula obconica*.

Paint the glass of your greenhouse with a special shade paint to control temperatures. Remember to paint the outside surface of the glass – painting the inside will keep sunlight out without reducing the heat inside.

Good growing conditions

Plants under glass often grow at an astonishing rate during summer, and need continuous care for the best results.

■ **Check their watering needs** morning and evening, more often in hot weather.

■ **Mist leafy plants regularly** to increase humidity and discourage red spider mite.

■ **Feed every seven to ten days** with a dilute liquid fertiliser.

■ **Water cacti and succulents** regularly and stand outdoors if you can. Position desert species in full sun and forest kinds, such as Christmas cacti, in light shade and with shelter from the wind.

Sowing for winter and spring

For pots of fragrant flowers in winter and spring, sow stocks, mignonette, schizanthus and cornflowers in a shaded coldframe.

Prick them out separately into small pots, and pot on in early autumn into 13–15cm (5–6in) pots for flowering.

Potting up arum lilies

The white arum, *Zantedeschia aethiopica*, will keep growing all year but others, such as the brilliant yellow *Z. elliottiana*, require a dry summer rest. Repot them all in August, when you can also remove young offsets and pot them separately in rich soil-based compost such as John Innes No. 3.

■ **Use 15–23cm (6–9in) pots** according to the size of rhizomes; position so the end buds are level with the surface.

■ **Stand pots outside** until early October, keeping them moist.

■ **Then bring them indoors** to a minimum temperature of 10ºC (50ºF). Higher temperatures will force earlier flowering.

Taking leaf cuttings/1

1 For African violets and gloxinias, pull or cut off a leaf stalk and shorten to 2–4cm (1–1½in) in length.

2 The leaves will root easily when placed in cuttings compost or a mix of equal parts of grit and perlite, with the base of each leaf just buried. Either cover with a clear plastic lid or stand in a closed and lightly shaded propagator. You can also root African violets by standing the leaves, with their stalks intact, in a jar of water.

Taking leaf cuttings/2

1 Several plants can be produced from a single leaf of *Begonia rex* when laid on the surface of compost. Cut off a leaf, then make cuts straight across the strongest main veins in a number of places, on the underside, using a sharp knife.

2 Spread the leaf, facing up, on the surface of a tray filled with cuttings compost or a grit and perlite mix. Weigh it down with pebbles and keep warm and moist in a propagator. Young plants will appear where the cuts touch the compost.

Forcing bulbs

You can force bulbs in pots and bowls to flower indoors in spring, or even earlier if you control temperatures carefully. For Christmas blooms, always choose prepared hyacinths, narcissi and tulips, and plant them no later than the third week in September. Choose a container at least 10cm (4in) deep. A 15cm (6in) wide bowl will hold three hyacinths, six narcissi or tulips, or 12 smaller bulbs such as crocuses. All bulbs need a cold but frost-free period to initiate root growth: allow about 12 weeks for narcissi and hyacinths, and 14–15 weeks for other bulbs.

Preparing Christmas plants

Poinsettias only start developing their colourful bracts once the flowers are initiated during a period of short days, which is why, left to their own devices, they flower in early spring. But you can trick them into flowering at Christmas by adjusting their growing conditions now.

■ **In early September,** keep your poinsettia at 17°C (63°F) or more and expose it to light for a maximum of ten hours each day, then cover it with a black plastic bag or move it into a dark cupboard for the remaining 14 hours. Do this for three weeks, then grow as normal in full light.

■ **Christmas cactus responds** to similar treatment, but needs about 12 hours of darkness per day for six weeks. Keep plants cooler, between 10–15°C (50–60°F).

Leaf cuttings

Some plants, such as *Begonia rex* (see left) and streptocarpus (see above right) can be grown from a leaf, or portions of it, and they can be propagated during summer. For streptocarpus, choose healthy, full-size leaves that are not too old and insert them vertically in pots or trays of moist cuttings compost. They will root in a few weeks. Pot up new young plantlets individually when they are large enough to handle.

Propagating streptocarpus

Streptocarpus can be propagated by leaf cuttings, in much the same way as *Begonia rex* (see left). Alternatively, you can slice the leaf sideways into several pieces, then bury the lower edge (the one nearest the parent plant) of each strip in the compost. Young plants will then grow from the cut veins.

Keeping the greenhouse cool

Temperatures under glass can soar alarmingly in late summer, and it is important to control this to ensure healthy plant growth and to protect foliage from scorching in the heat.

■ **Apply a further coat of shade paint** to the outside glass.

■ **Pull down the blinds;** consider fitting some if you haven't done so already.

■ **Cover seedlings with sheets** of newspaper on bright days.

■ **Open all doors and ventilators** to prevent temperatures from rising much above 20°C (68°F); do this at night too in exceptionally hot weather conditions.

■ **Damp down paths,** floor and staging daily with a hosepipe or watering can, especially if leaves look dull – a symptom of red spider mite infesting the underside of leaves.

■ **Water once, preferably twice,** daily, and watch out for early signs of water stress such as flagging or lacklustre leaves and a dry, stale smell as you enter the greenhouse.

Holiday tips

Before you go on holiday take precautions to prevent problems while you are away.

■ **Thoroughly water everywhere** the night before you leave if the weather is dry.

■ **Apply a thick layer of mulch** to drought-sensitive plants after soaking them.

■ **Water and feed plants,** and move them away from sunny windows to stand in self-watering containers or a bowl or sink of shallow water.

■ **Deadhead all fading flowers** and cut off an flowers that are fully open.

■ **Gather ripe fruit and vegetables,** together with any that are nearly ready.

■ **Get up to date with pricking out** and potting on so that young plants continue growing unchecked.

■ **Ensure there is adequate shading** and consider investing in an automatic ventilator and watering system.

Hover flies will be attracted by bright flowers in the greenhouse. Their larvae feed on any aphids.

■ **Arrange for a neighbour** or friend to water while you are away, and to pick ripening fruit and vegetables.

■ **Fit automatic ventilators** to open at least one top and one side window above a pre-set temperature.

■ **Get up to date with your potting** and planting before you go.

■ **Remove faded, discoloured** or dead leaves, especially from plants in pots.

■ **Feed all plants and spray** them with a systemic insecticide or suspend sticky traps above their foliage.

■ **Install an automatic watering** system, using capillary matting or drip tubes, and fill all reservoirs (see page 93). Alternatively, take plants outdoors and group them together in a shady place where rain can reach them, watering them thoroughly just before leaving.

Pest control

In the concentrated warmth and humidity of summer, pests and diseases can multiply rapidly in a greenhouse, so stay alert for early signs of infestation and take prompt action when a pest is identified. Simple, precautionary measures include keeping the atmosphere in the greenhouse humid to prevent red spider mites from spreading, hanging up sticky yellow cards as insect traps (see page 99), and keeping your plants in peak condition.

Aphids, whitefly, scale insects, red spider mites and vine weevils are the most common greenhouse pests. However, these can be kept under control simply by introducing a specific parasite or predator (see box, above right).

Biological controls are effective all season, but only if the pest is already present and the temperatures are high enough, so wait until you see the first signs in early summer. And remember, you cannot combine biological control with conventional spraying because the biological control will be killed by any insecticides.

Biological control methods

To control:	You need:
■ aphids	■ *Aphidius* parasite
■ red spider mite	■ *Phytoseiulus* parasite
■ scale insect	■ *Metaphycus* parasitic wasp
■ vine weevil	■ *Heterorhabditis* nematodes
■ greenhouse whitefly	■ *Encarsia* parasitic wasp

Cleaning the greenhouse

The most convenient time to clean out your greenhouse is on a mild day at the end of the season when most crops have finished and before you bring in tender plants for protection. Move any plants in pots outside before you start.

■ **Remove all used pots,** trays and labels. Clean and store them for later use. Clear out plant remains and brush down the inside structure and the staging to remove cobwebs, loose compost and ther debris.

■ **Wash inside the glass** using a cloth and warm water mixed with a little washing-up liquid and garden disinfectant; use a scrubbing brush or old toothbrush for the glazing bars. Clean dirt and algae from overlapping panes with a thin seed label. Rinse with a hosepipe or pressure sprayer and clean water.

■ **Repair any broken glass** and make good structural defects.

■ **Brush down staging** and scrub it with warm water and garden disinfectant.

■ **Wash surface gravel** on the staging with a pressure sprayer. Sweep and scrub solid floors with water and garden disinfectant, and hose them clean.

■ **Wash or scrub the outside** of the pots in use before putting the plants back in the clean greenhouse. Shut ventilators in the evening and fumigate the greenhouse with a smoke cone.

The coldframe in summer

Once you've hardened off tender plants you can still put the coldframe to good use.

■ **Use it as a seedbed** for sowing biennials and perennials or as a nursery bed for raising transplanted seedlings.

■ **Make it a bed for propagating** soft-tip and semi-ripe cuttings and divided plants.

Cleaning inside the greenhouse

1 After repairing broken panes, use a sponge to wash the glass with warm water mixed with washing-up liquid and garden disinfectant.

2 Brush down the staging with plenty of warm water and garden disinfectant.

3 Rinse it clean using warm water and a cloth.

Autumn

As the growing season comes to a close there is plenty of weeding and tidying to be done, but leave a few seed heads standing for their winter beauty. This is also a good time to lift and divide large clumps, as new plants will establish well in early autumn.

Autumn checklist

■ **Move tender perennials under cover** before the first frosts.

■ **Cut back to ground level** perennials that have died down, although there are benefits in delaying this job until spring (see below). Remove supports and destroy diseased growth.

■ **Mulch plants on the borderline** of hardiness (see opposite).

■ **Divide clumps** of established perennials, giving priority to those that flower in spring.

■ **Treat perennial weeds** such as bindweed with a systemic weedkiller.

■ **Look for self-sown seedlings** as you weed. Pot these up or transplant to a nursery bed for planting out next year.

■ **Move under cover** any young perennials growing in pots outside.

■ **Order new perennials** from mail-order suppliers, who will despatch them in a dormant state.

■ **Plant out new perennials** in September if possible, including polyanthus divided in early summer.

■ **Pot up rooted cuttings** and layers started in late summer.

■ **Prick out seedlings** sown in late summer into modular trays or small pots once they are large enough to handle, usually when the first pair of true leaves has formed.

■ **Collect seed when ripe** for sowing now or storing.

Cutting back perennials

Once the growth of perennials, ferns and ornamental grasses has died back to the ground it can be cut back to make your garden look tidy. However, there are benefits in delaying the traditional autumn tidy-up until late winter or early spring.

From an aesthetic point of view, the dead leaves and seed heads of many plants look beautiful when rimed with frost or bejewelled with pearls of moisture on a misty morning. The dead growth also gives the plant extra protection from the cold, and provides shelter for hibernating insects like ladybirds and lacewings, which are natural predators of garden pests such as aphids.

■ **Cut back lush-leaved plants** like hostas in autumn, as they quickly turn to mush.

■ **You must also cut back** any plants with diseased foliage. Remove and destroy the plant material. Do not leave it *in situ* – the disease spores could survive over winter – and do not put it on the compost heap.

Tender perennials These rarely tolerate frost and need to be moved under cover in autumn. Lift and pot up any plants growing in the border and move them into a well-lit, frost-free place such as a greenhouse, porch or conservatory. Plants in an unheated structure will often survive if the compost is kept on the dry side. However, if you have already rooted some cuttings to overwinter indoors, you could leave the parent plant outside to take its chances.

When applying a mulch on your beds, begin by covering any plants with an upturned flower pot or other container. This prevents the plants themselves getting covered with mulch.

Dividing geraniums

1 Lift the clump using a garden fork and shake off excess soil.

2 Insert two garden forks into the clump back-to-back and then lever apart. Repeat until plants are a good size. This is the best way to split fibrous-rooted plants like geraniums, michaelmas daisies and Japanese anemones.

3 Replant the small divisions into soil that has been refreshed with some well-rotted compost or manure and a handful of planting fertiliser. Ensure the plants are at the same depth as they were growing previously.

Weeding and mulching

Carry out these jobs between autumn and spring, when the ground is workable. Mulching now retains soil warmth, but clear the weeds first.

■ **Pull up annual weeds** and dig up the roots of perennial ones.

■ **Treat perennial weeds** with the systemic weedkiller glyphosate if it is not possible to dig out all the roots. Apply early in autumn so the plant draws the chemical down to its roots as it becomes dormant for the winter.

■ **Lay a mulch** 5–8cm (2–3in) deep of composted bark, cocoa shells, garden compost or well-rotted manure. Cocoa shells may help to repel slugs and snails.

■ **Plants of borderline hardiness,** such as penstemons, *Verbena bonariensis* and several salvias benefit from a thick, dry covering now in cold and exposed areas. Use materials such as leaves, bracken or straw, laid about 8cm (3in) thick. Put a few woody prunings over it or peg some chicken wire over the top to prevent the mulch from being blown away.

Dividing perennials

When your perennials are several years old and have formed established clumps they can be lifted while they are dormant in autumn or winter and divided into several pieces. Replant the divisions at the same depth. As long as each piece has a reasonable amount of roots and some buds, they will quickly form a new small clump.

■ **Wash off the soil** if you have trouble seeing the positions of roots and shoot buds.

■ **Discard the centre** if the clump has become unproductive and woody, and replant only the young outer portions.

■ **Hellebores and peonies** dislike being divided and take several years to settle down again, so these are best left undisturbed.

■ **Spring and summer-flowering** perennials are best divided in autumn so they have plenty of time to settle down before flowering next year.

■ **Late summer and autumn-flowering** perennials may be divided now or in early spring. In cold areas, delay dividing fleshy-rooted perennials like hostas until spring.

Autumn is a gamble. In a mild year continued deadheading can extend the flowering almost into winter, whereas a sudden frost may finish the display prematurely. Many summer bedding plants can be kept over winter, while there is still work to be done to ensure a good show next spring.

Autumn checklist

■ **Continue deadheading plants** regularly to prolong flowering for as long as the weather remains favourable.

■ **Thin late-summer sowings** of annuals so that plants stand 8–10cm (3–4in) apart. If you lift thinnings carefully with a fork they can be transplanted elsewhere or potted up for greenhouse display.

■ **Cut remaining flowers** if hard frost threatens, and use for indoor decoration.

■ **Remove faded and frosted plants** to the compost heap, weed and rake up fallen leaves so the ground is clear for replanting.

■ **Lift pelargoniums, argyranthemums** and other tender bedding perennials before the first frosts, and pot up or take cuttings ready for overwintering indoors (see below).

■ **Buy wallflowers** from a garden centre and plant immediately (see right).

■ **Plant out spring bedding** in display beds and other prepared areas (see opposite).

■ **Protect seedlings of hardy annuals** with cloches or fleece in the event of severe frost.

■ **Sow sweet peas indoors** for best results next spring (see page 126).

■ **Pot up some of the best** summer bedding plants – such as ageratums, busy lizzies, helichrysum and petunias – to keep over winter for spring cuttings.

■ **Gather and dry seeds** of favourite and unusual plants to store for spring sowing.

Overwintered bedding plants

Healthy summer bedding plants may be kept from one year to the next.

■ **Carefully lift some of the best** specimens of summer bedding before the first frosts and pot them up in 9–10cm (3½–4in) pots of soil-based compost.

■ **Trim the top growth** of the plants to about 5–8cm (2–3in) high and keep just moist in a frost-free greenhouse over winter.

■ **Increase heat and watering** in March to induce new growth suitable for soft-tip cuttings. The parent plants will often renew and make large specimens for planting out again next summer.

Many annuals flower well into autumn, especially if the weather remains mild. The blooms of *Cosmos bipinnatus* can be bright pink, mauvy pink or white. Sow the seeds of this half-hardy annual in spring, where they are to grow.

Planting wallflowers
1 Before planting them out, keep the bare-rooted plants in a bucket of water.
2 Several plants together make more of an impact than single spaced plants.

Wallflowers for next spring

Wallflowers are popular spring bedding that many gardeners prefer to buy as bare-rooted plants in autumn, rather than devote space to raising them from seed. Choose compact, branching plants with plenty of rich green foliage. Avoid buying thin, drawn specimens, which seldom bush out after planting, or plants with yellow leaves that indicate starvation or stress from being out of the ground too long.

Before planting, apply a little lime to the planting site unless your soil is naturally alkaline, as wallflowers are cabbage relatives and are similarly prone to club-root disease. Plant wallflowers immediately or heel in (bury) the roots in a spare piece of ground until you are ready.

Planting spring bedding

Traditional spring bedding displays combine edging plants around a central 'carpet' of wallflowers or forget-me-nots and bulbs such as tulips. Start planting once summer flowers have been cleared and try to finish the task before November.

Perennials as annual bedding

Although often treated as biennials, spring bedding plants such as polyanthus, primroses and double daisies (*Bellis*) are in fact perennials that can be multiplied and re-used year after year. Ideally, they should be divided frequently – at least every two years. Whether you started by raising your own from seed in May or June, or you bought the plants, you can dig up plants that have flowered in early summer and split them into smaller portions. Planted out in a nursery bed, in a humus-rich soil and moist shade, the segments will develop into full-size plants by autumn. You can now transplant them as part of the usual bedding routine ready for spring flowering.

Wallflowers are treated differently: tear off sideshoots from the best plants in late spring and use these as cuttings. Dip the bases in rooting hormone and root them under glass.

Planting spring bedding

1 Use a garden fork to clear away any weeds and to prick over the surface to aerate the soil. Rake the soil level and clear of debris, then leave the plot to settle for a few days.

2 Begin by planting the edging, spacing plants 15cm (6in) apart. Then plant the other bedding. Space plants closely, between 20–23cm (8–9in) apart, because little growth is made before flowering.

This is the time to plant spring-flowering bulbs in beds or borders, naturalise them in lawns or line them out in generous rows for cutting. As summer varieties die down, bring them indoors to dry, at about the same time as forced spring bulbs show their first fat buds.

Autmn checklist

■ **Continue planting spring bulbs** outdoors, such as daffodils, muscari, early crocuses, erythroniums, ornitholgalums and dwarf iris. Leave tulips and hyacinths until last (see below); finish planting by November.

■ **Plant large-flowered anemones** for flowers from January onwards (see right).

■ **Protect autumn-flowering bulbs,** such as amaryllis and nerines, from frost and heavy rain, particularly those growing in pots, by covering them with cloches, fleece or dry mulch.

■ **Lift begonias, dahlias and gladioli** before or after frosts (see opposite).

■ **Prepare new beds for gladioli,** selecting a well-drained position in full sun.

■ **Check that bulbs** potted for forcing for flowers in late winter or early spring are still sound and moist. Bring indoors any that are forward, with buds above soil level, but keep them cool.

■ **Lift, divide and replant** overcrowded clumps of alliums, summer snowflakes (*Leucojum*) and crocosmias. Collect seeds and bulbils for potting under glass.

■ **Propagate hyacinths** by scoring or scooping (see opposite).

■ **Propagate lilies** by scaling for forcing indoors (see opposite).

■ **Pot up arum lilies** for early flowering under glass if you have not done so already.

Planting tulips and hyacinths

Once you have planted daffodils and other bulbs that prefer an early start, you can turn your attention to hyacinths and tulips. For outdoor use, smaller 'bedding' hyacinths are preferable to the large bulbs sold for forcing. They can be left permanently in borders, although flower size may decline.

Dahlias provide bright colour in the garden well into autumn, especially in sheltered gardens. Cut plants back after they are blackened by the first frost and lift the tubers for winter storage.

For best results in spring bedding use fresh bulbs each year and space them about 20cm (8in) apart each way. Use old bulbs for propagation (see opposite).

The ideal time to plant tulips is late October or early November to prevent premature leaf growth and the risk of disease. Give them an open sunny position and plant them deep; 20cm (8in) is sufficient for most soils, but 30cm (12in) is better on light ground. Deep-planted bulbs can be left for three years or more, instead of being lifted annually, which is advisable if shallow planted. Space bulbs 10–20cm (4–8in) apart according to size, or plant more closely in layers in containers (see page 120).

Planting anemones

Plant two or three batches of large-flowered *Anemone coronaria* St Bridgid and De Caen Group between September and early November for a succession of colourful flowers to cut in spring.

■ **Soak the tubers** in water overnight, and then plant (with the 'claw' shapes pointing upwards) in rich soil, 5–8cm (2–3in) deep and 10cm (4in) apart in rows and blocks.

■ **For early blooms,** cover outdoor rows with cloches or plant some tubers in a coldframe or cool greenhouse.

Propagating from bulbs

Although hyacinths will naturally produce tiny bulblets, they are often extremely slow to multiply. You can speed up propagation by scoring the baseplate on any sound hyacinth (see below). In spring, small leaves will appear around the main bulb. Allow

Propagating with lily scales

1 Pull the small scales off lily bulbs after cleaning off the soil.
2 Plant them in a seed tray with their base just pushed down into the compost.

growth to die down in summer and remove the bulb from the pot. Up to a dozen bulblets will have formed, and these can be removed for growing on to flowering size.

Scooping is even more productive than scoring. Use a sharp knife to gouge or scoop out a cone of tissue from the baseplate, cutting about a quarter of the way into the bulb. Discard the cone of tissue, then dust the cut surface of the bulb with fungicide, pot up and grow on as for scoring.

Lifting summer bulbs

Many summer-flowering bulbs need to be brought indoors just before the frosty weather begins or as soon as the first frost has blackened the foliage. This can happen in early October some years, or well into November in a mild season.

■ **Dry bulbs for two to three weeks,** then carefully rub off all soil, roots and papery scales before packing them in dry compost in trays, boxes or bags. Store them in a dry, cool, but frost-free place.

TIP Lift begonias before the first frost and lift dahlias, crocosmias, gladioli, ixias and sparaxis after the first frost.

Scoring hyacinth bulbs

1 Clean off soil, roots and loose scales, then make two deep cuts across the base, almost a third of the way into the bulb; replant.
2 When bulblets have formed, pot them up with their tips at surface level. Grow on in a greenhouse or coldframe over winter.

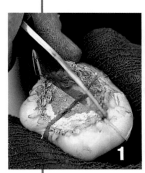

If the weather stays mild, roses will carry on flowering well into autumn. To prolong the display, continue with deadheading and disease control. The main task this season, however, is to plant new roses so that they have time to establish before winter sets in.

Autumn checklist

- **Plant or heel in** new bare-rooted roses as soon as they arrive (see opposite).
- **Water new roses** in a dry season, especially those planted against walls.
- **Continue watering roses** in outdoor containers, but reduce the frequency.
- **Tie in new growth on climbers** and ramblers, check their supports and shorten longer stems to reduce wind damage.
- **Prepare sites ready for planting** new roses (see opposite).
- **Continue spraying leaves** to guard against black-spot disease.
- **Tidy beds for winter** when roses have lost their leaves. Gather and remove or burn fallen leaves, clear away all weeds and lightly fork or hoe in surface mulches.
- **Protect newly planted roses** in cold areas.
- **Cut opening buds for the house** if frost threatens, deadhead faded flowers and remove developing hips to conserve the plant's energy, unless keeping for decorative reasons or for future propagation.
- **Pot up new roses** for forcing under glass.
- **Layer climbers, ramblers** and shrub roses (see below).
- **Continue deadheading** in a mild autumn, but remove only the flower, not a long-stemmed section as in summer.

Layering roses

You can layer any rose with flexible stems. They should be rooted by next autumn.
- **Choose a strong, flexible branch** that can be bent easily to meet the ground. Lightly fork over the soil at this position and work in a few handfuls of potting compost.
- **Cut into the underside** of the chosen branch, about 30cm (12in) from its tip, to make a 10cm (4in) long sliver of stem stick

out. Wedge this open with a thin twig and place that section on the loosened soil.
- **Peg the branch down** into the soil with a piece of bent wire.
- **Use a cane to support** the end of the branch protruding from the soil in an upright position; tie it in. Water well around the layer.

Success with roses

- **Roses will thrive** for many years if you prepare the ground well, plant carefully and then foster their positive health.
- **Roses prefer slightly acid soils.** Chalky soils and overliming can result in deficiencies of vital nutrients, indicated by yellowing leaves and weak growth. If you garden on chalk choose old shrub roses (damask and hybrid musk), as they are fairly lime-tolerant.
- **Cultivate soil thoroughly** and deeply. Roses like heavy soils, but these sometimes drain badly. Correct poor drainage before planting as waterlogging is lethal. Improve light soils to increase moisture retention and prevent summer drought.
- **Buy strong plants** with plenty of roots and healthy stems.
- **Choose disease-resistant varieties** if you prefer not to spray.
- **Plant with care:** too deep or shallow planting, inadequate firming, dry or damaged roots, overcrowding and planting under trees all lead to problems.
- **Prune for open growth,** so air can circulate, but avoid heavy pruning on shrub and floribunda roses. Clear away all prunings.
- **Feed with a high-potash** fertiliser; a high-nitrogen feed will encourage soft growth, vulnerable to pests and diseases.

Planting roses

Prepare the soil at least a month before planting by digging thoroughly, adding plenty of organic matter and allowing it to settle (see page 75). It is not too late to do this now, although you might have to tread the soil firm before preparing to plant.

Preparing to plant Just before you expect your bare-rooted roses to arrive, fork over the surface to break up any lumps and remove any weeds. Spread a dressing of rose fertiliser over the area, and fork or hoe it in. Finally, rake the site level and mark the position of the roses with short canes.

Sandy and silty ground can dry out quickly in summer and this will affect the flowering and good health of rose plants unless you take steps to make a light soil more moisture-retentive.

■ **Dig in ample supplies** of well-rotted manure, garden compost or leaf-mould to increase humus levels and also stimulate beneficial bacteria that aid root growth.

■ **Mulch established plants** lavishly with an 8cm (3in) layer of well-rotted manure every spring and feed plants in spring and midsummer, because light soils also lose nutrients quickly.

Planting bare-rooted roses The basic planting method is the same for all rose types (see below). On arrival, unpack the plants, check their condition and, if the roots are dry, stand plants in a bucket of water for an hour or two. If you cannot plant them immediately, heel them in to keep their roots moist until you are ready. If the weather is wet or cold, plants can stay heeled in until February without injury.

Planting a bare-rooted rose

1 Before planting, tidy and trim plants to size. Prune each stem back to three to five buds long (climbers and ramblers to about 1.2m/4ft) and remove any dead wood and weak growth. Trim 5–8cm (2–3in) off the end of each main root.

2 After placing the rose in the prepared site, check that the rose is at its original depth, with the bud joint (the bulge immediately above the roots) just below surface level. The hole should be large enough to take the roots comfortably when they are evenly spread out over a small mound of soil.

3 Carefully replace the excavated soil over the roots, a little at a time, shaking the plant from time to time to ensure soil fills all air pockets between the roots.

4 When the hole is filled, firm all round the plant using hands or feet, and level the surface.

There is much to be done this season, including tying in plants and checking that supports are sound. This will lay the foundations for trouble-free performance next year. When the weather is fair, autumn is also a good time to plant new climbers and to continue to take hardwood cuttings.

Autumn checklist

- **Check plant ties** and tie in any new shoots before the autumn gales.
- **Inspect layers and pot up** those that are well rooted. Take hardwood cuttings.
- **Cut back herbaceous climbers,** such as golden hop and the perennial pea, to ground level once growth has died back. Pull up annual climbers killed by the frost.
- **Trim self-clinging climbers,** if necessary, to keep growth well away from window frames, downpipes and guttering.
- **Prune late-flowering clematis,** such as *C. tangutica* and *C. viticella,* which are growing through conifers and evergreens, once they have finished flowering. Cut back to 60–90cm (2–3ft) to reveal the host plant.
- **Plant hardy climbers** and wall shrubs in well-prepared ground (see right).
- **Water newly planted climbers** if dry spells occur and give established plants a twice-weekly soaking.
- **Weed and mulch** around established plants to retain warmth and moisture.

Virginia creeper makes a striking display as its foliage turns red – an eye-catching subject for an autumn hanging basket.

Planting clematis against a wall

1 Take the plant out of its pot and tease the roots loose if they are spiralling around the rootball.

2 Position the clematis in the hole, spreading out any loose roots, so that the top of the rootball is 10cm (4in) below ground level. Then back-fill round the rootball, firm and water.

3 Using several short bamboo canes that have been stuck into the soil at an angle to the wall, spread out the plant's stems and tie them to the canes. Do this for all climbers whether they are self-clinging or not.

Trellis

Trellis is an extremely adaptable material to use in all sorts of sites around the garden. It transforms any surface as it is decorative in its own right even before the climbing plants become established. Most trellis is made of wood and comes in many different designs, styles and prices.

■ **Basic 'squared' trellis** is the most economical and comes in 1.8m (6ft) lengths in panel widths from 30cm–1.8m (1–6ft).

■ **More decorative styles** include panels with concave or convex tops, diamond lattice and panels open in the centre.

■ **Criss-crossed willow stems** suit an informal or cottage garden, but expanding willow trellis is not durable and may last only a couple of years.

■ **Mount trellis** to support climbers on walls and fences.

■ **Mount panels between stout fence posts** to act as a free-standing screen around a patio, as a divider within the garden or along the boundary instead of a solid fence.

■ **Fix trellis on top of low walls** or fences to raise their height, create privacy or expand the growing area for plants.

Erecting trellis on walls and fences

The most important point is to incorporate battens or blocks of wood to create a 3–5cm (1–2in) space between the trellis and the wall or fence to which it is fixed. This gap enables plant stems to twine around the trellis and allows air to circulate, which helps to prevent diseases. Birds often take advantage of the gap to build their nests.

Maintaining supports

Pay particular attention to wooded supports at soil level, where rotting is most likely to occur. It is sometimes possible to saw off the rotten part and insert the post into a metal post holder, hammered into the hole occupied by the old post. Otherwise, sink a concrete spur into a hole dug next to the existing post and bolt the two together.

Wire supports

Strong galvanised wire running through vine eyes provides an inexpensive alternative to trellis on walls and fences, and is especially useful where you plan to cover large areas with climbing plants or wall shrubs.

On walls

1 Hammer a flat vine eye into the mortar of the garden wall.

2 Run the wire horizontally so it follows the lines of mortar between the bricks and is, therefore, hardly visible. Space horizontal wires approximately 30cm (1ft) apart and vertical wires 1.8m (6ft) apart.

On fences

1 Fix screw-type vine eyes to the posts on fences or into wooden supporting posts.

2 Strain the wires between the vine eyes and tighten using pliers, or fit tension bolts to make sure there is no slack.

Many shrubs and trees look spectacular in autumn, with late-flowering species in bloom and brilliant foliage tints as the season closes. In the midst of this dramatic display, take time to think about planting, renovating and propagating new plants for the years ahead.

Autumn checklist

■ **Continue watering regularly** in a dry autumn. Concentrate on shrubs and hedges planted less than a year ago, and trees planted up to two years ago.

■ **Water container-grown** shrubs and trees in dry weather, but gradually reduce the frequency as autumn advances.

■ **Pot up rooted cuttings** and overwinter in a coldframe or cool greenhouse.

■ **Move rooted layers** to their permanent sites (see opposite).

■ **Transplant rooted hardwood cuttings,** taken last autumn, to their new homes.

■ **Protect new plants,** especially young evergreens, from cold winds.

■ **Leave faded flowerheads** on hydrangeas until early spring to protect their young shoots from severe weather.

■ **Prepare planting sites** for new hedges (see page 118).

■ **Plant new evergreen shrubs,** trees and hedges between early and mid-autumn for best results, but wait until next spring if your garden is cold or exposed.

■ **Start planting new deciduous trees,** shrubs and hedges in prepared sites (see page 118).

■ **Prune long shoots** of late-summer and early-autumn flowering shrubs to prevent damage in windy weather (see opposite).

■ **Take semi-ripe cuttings** of evergreens in early autumn and root in a coldframe. Suitable plants include privet, laurel, lavender and lonicera.

■ **Begin renovating** neglected deciduous hedges in late autumn (see opposite).

■ **Propagate new shrubs and hedges** from hardwood cuttings (see opposite).

■ **Collect ripe seeds** from trees and shrubs for sowing now, if exposure to frost is

The red, gold and yellow leaves of *Nyssa sylvatica* create a beautiful central display in the garden each autumn.

necessary for germination, or to store in a dry place until spring.

■ **Net holly branches** laden with berries to protect them from birds until Christmas.

■ **Prepare sites** for new trees and shrubs. Plant deciduous species between autumn and spring, but leave evergreens until spring if you cannot plant them by mid-autumn.

Renovating a beech hedge

1 Using hedge shears, prune the hedge evenly all over to 10–15cm (4–6in) less than the ultimate finished surface; this allows room for dense re-growth.

2 To reduce the size more severely, cut back one side now and wait for a year before you cut the other side.

Pruning late shrubs

Shorten long shoots of late-flowering shrubs such as *Buddleja davidii*, caryopteris, leycesteria and brachyglottis that might be damaged by strong winds. Complete the pruning in early spring when there is less risk of frost damage if a warm autumn has stimulated new growth. Leaving top growth in place protects plants and benefits wildlife.

Renovating neglected hedges

Cut back overgrown deciduous hedges, such as beech, hornbeam and hawthorn, between late autumn and the end of winter during frost-free weather. This restores their shape and fills in bare patches (see above). Feed in early spring to support new growth.

Propagation

Take hardwood cuttings of shrubs and check those taken last year. Move those that have rooted well to their growing positions.

Hardwood cuttings These are 20–30cm (8–12in) portions of ripe, firm stems that have grown this year, either cut just below a bud or pulled from the main stem with a thin strip, or heel, of old bark.

■ **Trim any ragged edges** from the heel, then root the cuttings in a sheltered position. (For evergreen cuttings, remove leaves from the lower portion.)

■ **Dig a V-shaped trench** 10cm (4in) deep, and fill with equal amounts of soil and grit.

■ **Push the cuttings into this mixture,** upright and about 15cm (6in) apart, so that only 5–8cm (2–3in) is visible.

■ **Firm gently with your foot,** water if the soil is dry and leave until next autumn.

Layers Flexible shoots pegged into the soil in spring or last autumn should have rooted by now. Young shoots are the most visible indication of success, but gently pull at the layer to test whether there is any resistance.

■ **Transplant a layer** with well-developed roots to its permanent prepared site by cutting the branch joining it to the parent plant, then lifting it carefully with a fork. Leave any unrooted layers for another year.

PLANTING SHRUBS AND TREES

Dig over sites for new shrubs, trees and hedges well before planting, so the ground has a month or two in which to settle. If you have no opportunity to prepare the whole area in advance, plant immediately after digging individual sites.

To prepare a site for a new hedge, mark out the position by digging a trench 60cm (2ft) wide, with the planting line down its centre. Prepare the ground several weeks in advance or immediately before planting. As you refill the trench after planting, loosen the soil on the sides, especially in heavy soil, to prevent it from becoming a drainage channel for the surrounding ground.

Planting from a container

Mark out the planting position and dig a hole large enough to allow for 10cm (4in) of planting mixture beneath and all round the rootball of the plant.

- **Thoroughly water the plant** and stand it in the hole to check its position before carefully removing the container.
- **Fill in around the rootball** with planting mix, firming it as you go with your fists or a trowel handle, and level the surface.
- **For trees, position a stake** on the leeward side (the side away from the prevailing wind) and drive it in at an angle of 45 degrees to avoid damaging the rootball. Secure with an adjustable tie.

Staking trees

Young trees need staking until their roots have anchored them securely in the ground. For trees with tall, slender trunks or large heads of evergreen foliage, drive in a long stake so the top reaches the lowest branch and secure with one or two tree ties. Use ties that place cushioning between the tree and stake, or pad the contact point with a wad of sacking.

Preparing for planting

1 If you are planting in a lawn or grassed area, mark out a circle about 1–1.2m (3–4ft) across. Lift the turf and set aside. Fork out any perennial weeds, then dig out the area to the depth of a spade blade. Stack this topsoil to one side. Use a fork to loosen the subsoil and work in some garden compost or leaf-mould. Chop up any turf and lay this grass side down in the hole.

2 Prepare a planting mixture in the following way. Mix in a bucket 2.5 litres (½ gallon) each of well-rotted manure and garden compost (or leaf-mould), plus 100g (4oz) each of seaweed meal and bone meal. Add to the heap of excavated topsoil and mix together with a fork.

3 Before planting the tree or shrub add enough of the planting mix to raise the shrub or tree to the right depth and fork in well.

Planting a bare-rooted shrub or tree

1 Dig out a hole large enough to take the roots comfortably when spread out, and check the depth so the soil mark on the stem is at ground level. For trees, drive in a vertical stake 8–10cm (3–4in) off-centre and on the lee side, away from the prevailing wind.

2 Hold the plant upright in position – this might be easier with two people – spread a few trowels of planting mix (see step 3, left) over the roots, and gently shake the plant up and down to settle the mix in place. Repeat this procedure and firm the plant lightly with your fist.

3 Half-fill the hole and gently tread firm. Check the plant is still at the correct depth and adjust this if necessary by adding or removing soil.

4 Back-fill the hole, firm again and level the surface. Attach a tree to its support with an adjustable tie fixed near the top of the stake.

Staking container-grown and bare-rooted trees

A SHORT STAKE is adequate for sturdy and short-stemmed trees. For bare-root trees, drive the stake in vertically to come a third of the way up the trunk; secure with a tie.

FOR CONTAINER-GROWN TREES, drive in a short stake at an angle after planting, so that it misses the rootball and can be attached to the tree at about 45cm (18in) above the level of the soil.

ALTERNATIVELY, drive in two short upright stakes 60cm (2ft) apart on opposite sides of the trunk, join with a horizontal batten and attach to the tree with an adjustable tie.

Keep the colour displays in your containers going until the first hard frosts, then plant some seasonal displays to add cheer during the gloom of winter. This is also the time to plant spring bulbs, and to tuck up tender plants so they can flourish again next summer.

Autumn checklist

■ **Clear out hanging baskets** and other containers of annual plants once flowering has finished. Compost the remains unless they show signs of pests or diseases, in which case remove or burn them.

■ **Inspect compost for vine weevil.** The creamy white, brown-headed grubs can cause considerable damage to the roots of container-grown perennials. Treat with the chemical imidocloprid or repot in fresh compost that contains the chemical.

■ **Store containers** that are not frost-proof in a shed or garage after cleaning.

■ **Move frost-tender perennials** and shrubs under cover before the first frost. Keep them in a greenhouse or conservatory that is heated sufficiently to remain frost-free.

■ **Plant up containers** for autumn colour (see below).

■ **Plant bulbs** such as tulips for spring flowers (see opposite).

■ **Check containers** every couple of days and water the compost sparingly if this is necessary.

■ **Plant up containers** for winter colour.

Planting autumn containers

Planting containers at this time of year means paying even more attention than usual to good drainage, for compost that is soggy and poorly drained is liable to freeze in winter and kill or damage the plants, particularly bulbs. Avoid using potting compost containing water-retaining gel. You should also mass plants closely together to ensure a full display as there will be little growth between now and spring.

■ **Put in a layer of drainage** material about 5cm (2in) deep. Pieces of broken pots, or 'crocks', are ideal, but large stones or

Good drainage is essential. Add crocks, large stones or broken up polystyrene to the pot. Cover this with a layer of fine plastic netting, otherwise compost will fill the gaps and prevent water draining away.

chunks of broken up polystyrene trays are also suitable.

■ **Lay fine plastic netting** over the top of the crocks to prevent the spaces becoming clogged with compost.

■ **Part-fill the container** with a free-draining potting compost. Then pack the plants closely into the container so that they are all at the same depth as they were growing previously.

■ **Leave at least a 1cm (½in) gap** between the top of the compost and the rim to allow room for watering.

■ **Firm the compost lightly** and water it well. Stand the container on pot feet or pieces of tile so that excess water is able to drain away freely.

Bulbs for spring flowers

Few things liven up a patio in spring better than containers of bulbs, and autumn is the time to get planting. Daffodils, small narcissi and early flowering bulbs like crocuses need to go in as soon as possible, preferably by the end of September so they have enough time to establish a good root system. Tulips, on the other hand, are best planted in late autumn to avoid several diseases that could strike if the bulbs have been sitting in the compost for longer.

To create a really eye-catching display, plant different bulbs in layers in a deep container at least 30cm (12in) deep and 30cm (12in) across. A pot this size will accommodate 8–10 daffodils bulbs, 10–12 tulips or 15–18 crocuses.

Protect pots from the worst of the winter frost and rain in a coldframe or unheated greenhouse. Otherwise, stand them in a sheltered spot against the house wall, and tuck bubble plastic, straw or leaves around the pots to protect them from frost. Give the warmest spot to hyacinths as they are most likely to suffer from the cold.

TIP Make a cover of chicken wire to sit on top of large containers to protect newly planted bulbs against cats and squirrels.

Empty pots that held annual displays once they have finished flowering. Either wash the containers and store them in a shed or garage, or plant them up for autumn or spring colour.

Planting bulbs in a large container

1 Prepare your pot with a layer of crocks topped with around 5–8cm (2–3in) potting compost, then place the largest bulbs, usually tulips or daffodils, so their tops will be covered by 15cm (6in) of compost. Space them closely but so they do not touch, and cover them with a little compost.

2 Position medium-sized bulbs between the tulips, and add more compost. Finish off with small bulbs like crocus, dwarf narcissi or muscari, then cover with a 5cm (2in) layer of compost. Water after planting, then periodically.

With less use likely in the winter months ahead, autumn is the best time to repair damaged turf as well as preparing your lawn to withstand the colder weather. The grass needs mowing less frequently as temperatures drop, but there are fallen leaves and wormcasts to sweep up.

Autumn checklist

■ **Mow grass less frequently** and raise the height of the cutting blade.

■ **Disperse unsightly wormcasts** by brushing the lawn with a stiff broom or a besom before you mow.

■ **Apply autumn fertilisers,** which are high in phosphates and potash. This slows down the topgrowth of the grass and encourages better root development. Choose a day when the grass is dry and the soil is moist, especially where powder or granular formulations are used, so that they fall off the grass blades and onto the soil.

■ **Make repairs** to damaged lawns by reseeding bare patches and renewing broken edges (see opposite).

■ **Aerate the lawn** if drainage is poor or moss is a problem; top-dress to relieve compaction (see opposite).

Leaves will create bare patches if they are not removed with a lawn rake. Stack them in a corner to rot down into leaf-mould.

■ **Make a last effort** to eradicate moss and weeds before winter sets in.

■ **Rake up fallen** leaves regularly.

■ **Sow new lawns or lay turf** on soil well prepared in advance. The relatively warm, moist soil and the likelihood of air temperatures dropping as winter approaches, mean that root development is rapid and leaf growth is slow and steady, so a new lawn laid in autumn will be well established in time for next spring.

■ **Look out for toadstools** and other fungi. This is the time of year they are visible, even though they may be present in the soil all year round. Most are harmless and just feed on organic matter in the soil, but brush them off if you wish.

Mowing

Grass continues to grow while the soil is still relatively warm and moist, but with the first frosts it starts to show signs of slowing down; it is only when the soil temperature drops below 5–7°C (41–45°F) that the grass stops growing for the winter. Before that time, it helps to leave the grass longer to protect the base of the plants from early frosts. Once it shows no signs of growth, cease mowing until the spring.

■ **Mow less frequently:** once a week should be sufficient in autumn.

■ **Raise the cutting blade** of the mower to 2–4cm (1–1½in).

■ **Remove all grass clippings** from the lawn as they will encourage the development of moss and worm activity.

TIP If the grass is too wet to cut and you have a hover mower, remove the blades (or put the mower on its highest setting) and run it over the lawn to 'blow dry' the grass. Then you can mow the grass.

Clearing leaves

If leaves are allowed to accumulate on the lawn for more than four or five days without being removed, the grass will suffer. Moss is encouraged by the dark, moist conditions under the leaves.

Rake up the leaves and use them to make leaf-mould. You can also use your mower to help clear leaves and mow the grass at the same time: a light covering of leaves can be chopped by the mower and collected in the grass box. Add the mixed leaves and grass to the compost heap.

Relieving compaction

The main cause of many lawn problems is soil compaction. This is usually caused by regular activity – such as sport – or traffic on the lawn, which presses air out of the soil. The resulting lack of air causes the grass to die from the roots up, leaving sparse or bald patches, unless you take steps to alleviate compaction.

■ **Spike the lawn** with a border fork every 15–20cm (6–8in) to a depth of 15cm (6in). Even better is to use a hollow-tine spiker, which allows more air round the grass roots as it takes out small plugs of turf, which can be swept up and composted.

■ **Fill the holes** by brushing in a top-dressing to encourage new roots to form. On clay or poorly drained soils use a mixture of one part peat (or peat alternative), two parts loam or good-quality topsoil and four parts horticultural sand.

Repairing broken edges

The most vulnerable areas of a lawn are the edges, which can easily become ragged or damaged by walking or mowing. If they are left alone, damaged edges will gradually crumble away and spoil the overall appearance of the lawn. Eventually you will need to re-cut the lawn, reducing its area. Far better is to repair damage in the early stages. The site of the repair should be invisible within six weeks.

Repairing a lawn edge

1 Place a plank on the lawn to act as a guide and cut out the damaged turf using a half-moon edging tool. Using a spade, cut horizontally under the turf at a depth of about 5cm (2in), severing the grass roots.

2 Lift out the turf and rotate it 180 degrees so the damaged edge is within the lawn and the neat edge is on the outside edge. Firm the turf until it is just higher than the rest of the lawn; it will settle over the next few months.

3 Fill the gap that has been caused by the damaged area with fine garden soil; firm. Sow seed and water it in.

With shortening days and falling temperatures, the greenhouse offers a safe haven from conditions outdoors. Make preparations and organise the staging now for an influx of tender plants that need to share frost-free space with rooting cuttings and fresh sowings.

Autumn checklist

■ **Reduce watering and feeding** as growth slows. Stop damping down, only water in the mornings and avoid wetting foliage to prevent fungal diseases, which thrive in a damp atmosphere.

■ **Open ventilators** on mild days, but keep them closed during frost or fog.

■ **Allow permanent plants** more space, to improve air movement between them.

■ **Remove shade netting and paint** and wash down the outside of the glass. Shield young seedlings from bright sunshine with sheets of newspaper or a layer of fleece.

■ **Pot up seedlings of annuals** and other plants sown in late summer.

■ **Pot up well-rooted cuttings** of tender perennials and other plants propagated in late summer.

■ **Sow hardy annuals,** prick out into trays and overwinter in a coldframe.

■ **Sow sweet peas** in deep pots of seed compost or paper tubes.

■ **Lift and dry bulbs and tubers** ready for their winter rest (see page 111).

■ **Pot up lilies in deep pots** for flowering in their containers or for transplanting outdoors in spring.

■ **Make space for tender perennials** that have stood outdoors during summer before the first frosts come. First scrub the outsides of the pots and check the plants for any evidence of insect infestation.

■ **Stop watering cacti** to keep them dry and safe from frost.

■ **Pot up some hardy perennials** such as astilbes, aquilegias, dicentras and hellebores, to flower early indoors.

■ **Check for pests,** especially whitefly and red spider mite, and spray with insecticide. It is too late to introduce biological controls, which are only effective in warm conditions.

■ **Pick off fading leaves,** dead flowers and any sign of decay or mould, to reduce the risks from fungal diseases.

■ **Clean and sort pots.** Clean out gutters and water butts or tanks when leaves have finished falling (see page 126).

■ **Pot up spring bulbs** for indoor displays.

■ **Bring potted spring bulbs** into light and warmth when shoots reach 5cm (2in) high.

■ **Move potted herbs inside** to keep the kitchen supplied during winter.

■ **In late autumn insulate** the greenhouse (see page 127), and test heaters before they are needed. If you plan to install heating, decide on the types of plants you are likely to grow and the temperature regime they prefer.

■ **Make repairs** to the greenhouse and coldframes before winter.

■ **Clean the greenhouse** before it fills up with tender plants.

Empty containers or those that are not frost-hardy need to be stored in a shed or garage during the winter. Clean them thoroughly ready for reuse in spring.

As temperatures start to drop in autumn it is time to bring some of the less hardy plants into the greenhouse.

Sweet peas from seed

For top-quality blooms sow sweet peas in deep pots of moist soil-based seed compost during mid-October. Stand the pots in a coldframe or unheated greenhouse, and ventilate well in mild weather. Keep the seedlings in a coldframe until March, when they can be planted out.

You can also raise sweet peas in home-made paper tubes (see right). This method avoids any root disturbance because the tubes stay in the tray over winter and are planted out intact; the paper disintegrates.

Preparing for winter

The autumn clean-up in preparation for overwintering tender plants is a good opportunity to wash pots and cloches. Used plant containers can be a source of disease if they are left in a dirty condition under the greenhouse staging. Water butts and gutters also benefit from a scrub so they do not become a source of damping-off disease and other problems. Don't forget to wash the outside of the glass as light levels fall and you fix up winter insulation.

Cleaning equipment

■ **Examine your containers.** Mend cracks and breaks in large clay pots with strong, waterproof glue then place a tight wire hoop round the outside for reinforcement. Discard broken, cracked or brittle plastic containers. Repair wooden trays and boxes with slats, perhaps from an old fence panel or pallet.

■ **Scrub pots and trays** in warm soapy water with added horticultural disinfectant. Use a stiff washing-up brush to get well into the corners and under rims, where pests often hide. There is no need to scrape chalky deposits from clay pots, but do remove all traces of green algae.

■ **Dry containers thoroughly** before packing away according to size. Keep clay and plastic pots separate. Paint wooden trays with diluted horticultural disinfectant or a wood preservative.

Sowing sweet peas in paper tubes

1 Fold a sheet of newspaper or pages from an old telephone directory to make a long strip about 10cm (4in) wide. Roll this round a rolling pin or thick piece of dowel and fasten with sticky tape. Then slide off the paper tube.

2 Pack the tubes in a seed tray so they stand upright. Use a plastic funnel to fill them with compost and sow two seeds in each tube, about 1cm (½in) deep. Stand the tray in a little water until the top of the compost is moist.

3 When seedlings have four pairs of leaves, remove the weaker plant and pinch out the tip of the other to encourage strong sideshoots.

Remove leaves from greenhouse gutters that supply water butts.

■ **Plastic labels are re-useable.** If you soak them in a container filled with a diluted bleach solution they will be easy to scrub clean with a scourer or wire-wool pad. Rinse and spread out to dry.

■ **Drain water tanks and rain butts** and scrub the insides with warm soapy water and disinfectant. Rinse well before re-filling.

■ **Clear leaves from roof gutters** and clean with disinfectant to prevent disease.

TIP Clean and wash coldframes and cloches now, before their main season of use.

Insulating the greenhouse

About 80 per cent of heat in a greenhouse is lost through the glass, but you can reduce this by insulating the inside from late September or October until April.

Double glazing is the most efficient way to conserve heat, but it is expensive and only a serious option for a conservatory that is also used as a living area. A far cheaper method is to line the greenhouse inside with a skin of clear polythene sheeting, pinned to the glazing bars or attached with special plastic

Saving heat

■ Insulate the greenhouse after cleaning and drying the glass.

■ Seal gaps to reduce draughts. Repair cracked and broken glass, and fill holes with clear silicon sealant. Make sure the door fits well, but do not make the greenhouse totally draught-proof because some air movement is essential for reducing condensation.

■ Save up to ten per cent of heat by insulating the floor. You can do this by laying plastic sheeting underneath paving, spreading gravel over a woven geotextile membrane, or simply covering the floor with a temporary carpet of bark.

■ Group plants that need extra warmth at one end of the greenhouse, lined with thick insulation and separated off by a curtain of fleece or polythene. Cover seedlings and small tender plants with propagator lids. Move larger tender plants onto windowsills indoors.

■ Keep newspapers handy for covering plants on cold nights.

■ Draw down external roller blinds at night to trap heat in.

clips to leave a 2–3cm (1in) air gap. This can save 30 per cent of the heat lost. By using bubble plastic for lining, the saving increases to 40 per cent. Thicker materials save even more heat, but reduce light levels proportionally. An effective compromise is to use thick, triple-layer bubble plastic with large bubbles for the lower half of the walls, and thinner material above bench level.

Instead of insulating the roof, install a thermal screen above head height to pull across on horizontal wires at night and on cold days. Use fleece, clear woven plastic or a similar porous material to reduce condensation, which is sometimes a problem with polythene-sheet insulation.

TIP Remember to trim and fix insulation materials around ventilators so that these can be opened during mild weather.

Winter

Most perennials become dormant in winter, which makes the few that flower or hold their leaves an especially welcome sight in the garden. Lift your spirits in the winter months by bringing on new plants for the year ahead, either from plug plants or from root cuttings.

Winter checklist

■ **Plant bare-rooted perennials** such as lily of the valley, which are sold dormant, usually by mail order, at this time of year.

■ **Buy and pot up young plants,** or 'plugs', in late winter. Grow them on in a coldframe or an unheated greenhouse.

■ **Protect perennials** on the borderline of hardiness in cold or exposed gardens.

■ **Group pot-grown plants** together in a sheltered spot to reduce the risk of their rootballs freezing.

■ **Check new plants** put in during autumn and refirm any lifted by frost.

■ **Look for vine weevil larvae** in the compost of container-grown perennials if you suspect damage.

■ **Pick off old and tattered foliage** of early flowering evergreen perennials, such as bergenias, Lenten rose (*Helleborus orientalis*) and epimediums, in late winter.

■ **Protect flowers for cutting** of Christmas rose and *Iris unguicularis* from severe weather and bird damage, using cloches, sheets of glass or rigid plastic on bricks.

■ **Prepare new borders** for spring planting during fair weather. Dig them over to two spades' depth, incorporating plenty of well-rotted organic matter. Be sure to bury annual weeds and remove the roots of perennial weeds.

■ **Remove and clean plant supports,** and store ready for spring. Paint metal supports if necessary.

■ **Divide large clumps** of summer-flowering perennials and herbaceous climbers in late winter, so long as the ground is not frozen or waterlogged (see page 107).

Japanese anemone (*Anemone* x *hybrida* 'Géante des Blanches'), a delight in the autumn border, can be propagated by root cutting.

■ **Divide container-grown perennials** that have outgrown their pots, but delay dividing pot-grown grasses until early spring.

■ **Take root cuttings** (see below).

■ **Water tender perennials** overwintering under glass occasionally, to keep compost just moist. Check plants once a week, and remove dead leaves and flowers that could become infected with grey mould (botrytis).

■ **Top-dress** container-grown plants.

■ **Weed, tidy and mulch borders** in late winter, cutting dead stems to ground level.

Root cuttings

This is a useful way to propagate perennials with thick, fleshy roots (see below). The cuttings can be left outdoors, although standing them in a coldframe is preferable. In spring or early summer, when leaves appear, pot up the cuttings individually and grow them on for planting outside in autumn or the following spring. Replant the parent plant immediately into soil you have improved by forking in well-rotted organic matter and a little slow-release fertiliser.

Taking root cuttings

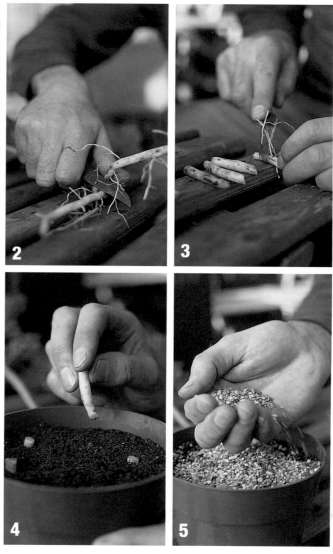

1 Dig up a strong, healthy plant and wash the soil off the roots.

2 Select young, vigorous pencil-thick roots and cut from the parent plant near the crown.

3 Cut each root into 7–10cm (3–4in) lengths, cutting straight across the top and slanting at the bottom (so you know which way up to plant them).

4 Fill a deep 13cm (5in) pot with moist cuttings compost. Insert six to eight cuttings round the rim, 2–5cm (1–2in) apart, their tops level with the surface.

5 Cover the compost with a fine layer of grit and place the pots in a coldframe, a sheltered place outdoors, or on the windowsill of a cool room.

Now is the perfect time to plan your planting schemes for next spring. Take some time to peruse the catalogues now available for new varieties and colours. Check biennials are still in good condition after spells of harsh weather and start sowing half-hardy annuals under glass.

Winter checklist

■ **Clear beds** where late annual displays have finished. Weed, then cover the ground with a layer of garden compost, ready to be forked in early in spring.

■ **Check biennials after bad weather** and firm in plants loosened by winds and frost. Remove any that are severely frosted, but do not replace them until early spring.

■ **Thin autumn-sown seedlings** to leave young plants at least 5cm (2in) apart as a precaution against damping-off disease.

■ **Cover seedlings** and young plants with cloches, fleece, polythene tunnels or newspaper in very cold weather.

■ **Plan next year's display** by exploring catalogues. Order seeds early to ensure a wide selection of varieties.

■ **Start cultivating sites** for annuals towards the end of winter when the weather is fair (see page 19). Prepare a small area of ground as a nursery bed in which to sow hardy annuals for transplanting. Delay this until early spring in a wet season or if your soil is heavy clay.

■ **Sow half-hardy annuals under glass** from January onwards, and prick them out when they are large enough to handle.

■ **Place your orders** for seedlings and plug plants in February for spring delivery; this is often an easier and less expensive alternative to raising your own from seed in a heated greenhouse.

■ **Pot up seedlings** sown in autumn under glass, and grow them on in a greenhouse or coldframe for early flowers indoors.

Winter-flowering pansies grown in pots or containers are one of only a few annuals to provide a splash of colour this season.

Choosing annuals

Besides the many popular annuals, such as pot marigolds, French marigolds, ageratums and salvias, that are happy in a sunny position in most garden soils, the following plants will suit particular requirements:

For cutting ▪ antirrhinum ▪ calendula ▪ china aster ▪ chrysanthemum ▪ gypsophila ▪ larkspur ▪ molucella ▪ nigella ▪ scabious ▪ sunflower ▪ sweet peas ▪ verbena

For fragrance ▪ alyssum (*Lobularia*) ▪ evening primrose ▪ heliotrope ▪ mignonette ▪ mirabilis ▪ nicotiana ▪ petunia ▪ stocks ▪ sweet peas

For foliage ▪ amaranthus ▪ atriplex ▪ *Begonia semperflorens* (bronze-leaved varieties) ▪ castor oil plant (*Ricinus*) ▪ coleus ▪ kochia ▪ nasturtiums (*Tropaeolum* Alaska Series) ▪ variegated pelargoniums ▪ perilla

For shade ▪ alyssum (*Lobularia*) ▪ begonias ▪ cleome ▪ coleus ▪ impatiens ▪ lobelia ▪ mimulus ▪ nicotiana ▪ pansies ▪ schizanthus

For meadows ▪ borage ▪ candytuft ▪ clarkia ▪ corncockle ▪ cornflower ▪ cosmos ▪ eschscholzia ▪ larkspur ▪ nasturtiums ▪ pansies ▪ poppies ▪ sunflowers

For climbing ▪ *Cobaea scandens* ▪ *Eccremocarpus scaber* ▪ morning glory ▪ sweet peas ▪ *Thunbergia alata* ▪ trailing nasturtiums

Quick fillers ▪ candytuft ▪ chrysanthemums ▪ linaria ▪ nigella ▪ night-scented stocks

Bring warmth to the garden with *Eschscholzia californica*.

Raising lobelia from seed

1 Fill a seed tray with moist seed compost and lightly firm and level. Use a pencil or thin cane to press parallel grooves about 1cm (½in) deep in the compost. Sow seeds sparingly along these channels but do not cover with compost as light is essential for germination. Cover the tray with some polythene or a clear lid and stand in a warm place.

2 When the seedlings are about 1cm (½in) high, fill another tray with moist potting compost, and make holes about 5cm (2in) apart. Lift small clumps of seedlings with a dibber and transfer to the holes in the new tray.

3 Lightly firm with your fingers, water through a fine rose, then put the tray in a propagator or cover it with a clear lid.

In containers and outdoors, the first flowers will be opening before the turn of the season. While you are enjoying these harbingers of the new year, get ahead with sprouting summer bulbs and preparing their ground. This will ensure that you experience the longest possible display.

Winter checklist

■ **Clear leaves and other debris** from around the shoots of snowdrops, scillas, muscari and other early bulbs. Do not fork or hoe the surface as this can cause damage.

■ **Protect buried bulbs,** especially tulips, from mice and squirrels. Lay panels of chicken wire on the ground and secure at the corners with large stones or bent wires.

■ **Move or divide snowdrops** while they are in flower or have green leaves (see below).

■ **Cover spring bulbs with cloches** or a low polythene tunnel to advance flowering if you planted them in rows for cutting. Ventilate on mild days to keep them free from rot.

■ **Start moving forced bulbs** into light and gentle warmth in December, no more than 10°C (50°F); hyacinths should have plump shoots with buds visible, and narcissi should be about 10cm (4in) high, with visible flower buds. Tulips and crocuses are often not ready until late January or February, when they show flower colour.

■ **Remove dead blooms** after flowering, then feed with a high-potash fertiliser. Move plants to a coldframe or sheltered position outside to continue growing and storing food to fuel next year's display.

■ **Buy lilies** for pots or outdoors. Refresh any that look dry and shrivelled by burying them in a tray of leaf-mould or moist compost for a week or two before planting.

■ **Pot up amaryllis** a few at a time for a succession of blooms (see opposite).

Moving snowdrops

1 Large clumps of snowdrops can be lifted with a fork while they are still in flower ('in the green').

2 Tease into smaller clumps and replant immediately in ground you have already forked over and enriched with leaf-mould or compost.

Planting amaryllis

1 Part fill a pot a little larger than the amaryllis bulb with moist potting compost so the bulb sits with its tip above the rim. Fill round the bulb with compost to within 2–3cm (1in) of the rim, then water.

2 Do not water again until the flower bud shows, then keep just moist.

3 When in flower, water plants regularly and feed every 7–14 days with liquid fertiliser.

■ **Carefully empty pans of lilies** propagated two years ago from seed or bulbils. These are usually large enough to separate and pot up individually in small pots. Leave one-year-old bulbs for another year.

■ **Prepare sites during February** for summer-flowering bulbs, such as gladioli, alliums, lilies and tigridias. Fork the ground thoroughly, removing perennial weeds and mixing in plenty of leaf-mould or garden compost. Delay this work until spring on frosted, wet or heavy soils.

■ **Sprout begonias and dahlias** in boxes under glass, either for taking cuttings in early spring or planting out in late spring.

If your lily bulbs look dry and shrivelled, place them in a pot or tray and cover with moist compost to plump them up.

With their blooms all gone, roses enjoy a rest. Some, however, develop vibrant hips that continue to add colour to the garden during their winter dormancy. You can plant or move roses now and, as winter draws to an end, prune them to concentrate their energy for the coming season.

Winter checklist

■ **Continue tidying rose beds.** Cut back any ground-covering herbaceous perennials and edging plants around the roses, clear weeds and pick up all fallen rose leaves.

■ **Give plants a final spray of fungicide** if black spot, rust or mildew have been a serious problem during the year. Choose a mild December day, drenching all stems to the point of run-off.

■ **Check recently planted roses** after frost and tread firm any that have lifted from the ground. If it gets very cold, cover young plants with straw.

■ **Continue preparing the ground** for new roses. In January, break down with a fork heavy soil roughly dug in autumn, ready for planting in late winter.

■ **Plant new roses as they arrive,** or heel them into some vacant ground until you are

Vibrant red rose hips add a colourful touch to the winter garden, as well as providing food for birds. Don't prune these varieties until spring.

ready. Plant only when the soil breaks up easily and is not frozen or waterlogged.

■ **Protect roses of borderline hardiness** with two or three layers of fleece. Varieties sensitive to frost include the banksian roses (*R. banksiae* cultivars), *R.* x *odorata* 'Mutabilis' and, in exposed positions, the yellow climber 'Mermaid'.

■ **Inspect supports and ties,** especially after high winds, and readjust where necessary (see page 141).

■ **Start pruning climbing roses** during February, but delay the work until March in a cold or frosty season.

■ **Move potted roses** into the greenhouse during January for forcing early blooms.

■ **Increase the resistance** of roses that have been badly affected by black spot in February by spreading 35g per m^2 (1oz per sq yd) sulphate of potash over soil shaded by the branches.

■ **Begin pruning shrub roses** in mild areas (see page 28).

Pruning climbing roses

Healthy climbers will have produced several new shoots during the summer. Retain the best and strongest of these when pruning to replace some of the older framework stems being cut out, or to fill in gaps.

Dealing with rose-sick soil

Where a rose has been grown for eight years or more, a replacement planted in the same spot is likely to grow sickly, with stems dying back. This is due to specific replant disease, or 'rose sickness', a combination of soil exhaustion and a build-up of diseases. It is better to plant a new rose somewhere fresh, but you can replant successfully in the same spot if you either replace the soil (see below) or use a soil-sterilising concentrate.

Replacing rose-sick soil

1 Dig out an area roughly 60cm (2ft) square around where the old rose grew, removing the top 38–45cm (15–18in) of soil. This soil is fine for growing other plants, so exchange it for the same amount dug from an area where roses have not been grown before.

2 Using a fork, work plenty of garden compost or well-rotted manure into the replacement soil at the planting site.

3 Leave the soil to settle for a few weeks before planting a new rose or moving one from elsewhere in the garden.

Now deciduous climbers are dormant, it is a good opportunity to see what lies beneath their cloaks of growth and tidy accordingly. This is the best season to prune certain climbers and service their supports. During very cold spells, evergreen and slightly frost-tender climbers will benefit from protection.

Winter checklist

■ **Protect climbers** on the borderline of hardiness during cold, frosty periods. If any leaves or shoots become damaged by frost, don't remove them but leave them in place until early spring because, although they appear unsightly, they give protection to undamaged shoots below.

■ **Continue to plant hardy climbers** when the soil is workable, and not frozen or sodden (see page 114).

■ **Lift and divide herbaceous climbers** that have formed well-established clumps (see page 107).

■ **Propagate selected climbers** by layering or taking hardwood cuttings in late winter (see page 140).

■ **Prune ornamental vines,** winter jasmine, wisteria and any overgrown deciduous climbers (see opposite).

■ **Check trellis and other supports** before growth begins, and repair or treat if necessary (see page 141).

■ **Tie in climber stems** firmly to avoid wind damage, and loosen existing ties if they threaten to cut into stems.

■ **Trim self-clinging climbers** away from woodwork and guttering.

■ **Occasionally water climbers** that are growing in sites that are sheltered from rain, such as beneath the overhanging eaves of a roof.

■ **Weed and mulch** carefully around established plants.

The star-shaped flowers of winter jasmine brighten the garden. Once flowering is finished, prune to promote the growth of new shoots that will carry flowers the following winter.

Pruning deciduous climbers

Early winter is the time to prune ornamental vines (*Vitis*), when pruning cuts are least likely to 'bleed' sap. Prune back weak or thin stems hard to encourage more vigorous growth; prune strong growing stems lightly.

Prune winter jasmine (*Jasminum nudiflorum*) as soon as flowering has finished because next winter's flowers open on new shoots produced during the coming year (see opposite).

Hard pruning ornamental vines whi e dormant will stimulate vigorous new growth in spring.

You can also prune overgrown deciduous climbers that will bloom on new wood produced in the coming year, such as trumpet vine (*Campsis*), summer jasmine (*Jasminum officinale*) and honeysuckle (*Lonicera periclymenum*). Late-flowering clematis are better left until early spring unless February is particularly mild.

Winter-pruning wisteria

Wisteria is pruned twice a year: around midsummer, then again in winter to

Winter pruning wisteria encourages the formation of short, flower-bearing sideshoots.

stimulate the formation of short sideshoots that will bear summer flowers. Plants left unpruned put their energy into producing leafy growth, not flowers.

■ **Cut back to two or three buds** the sideshoots that were shortened to five or six buds from the main stem in summer.

■ **Cut back any long shoots** that have developed to 15cm (6in).

■ **Feed it** with sulphate of potash towards the end of winter if it is shy to flower.

Pruning winter jasmine

1 Once flowering has finished, cut back all sideshoots that have borne flowers to around three buds from the main stem.

2 If necessary, shorten the main framework shoots to restrict growth.

3 On well-established plants, take out several of the older, more woody stems close to ground level.

Planting climbers

Winter is the time not only to propagate more climbers and check their supports, but also to plant new ones. One of the most beautiful combinations is a climber growing up through the branches of an established tree, giving an extra season of colourful flowers or foliage.

Propagation

There are various methods of propagating climbers at this time of year. Mature herbaceous climbers, such as golden hop, perennial pea (*Lathyrus latifolius*) and flame flower (*Tropaeolum speciosum*), are divided in the same way as herbaceous perennials when soil conditions are suitable.

Many deciduous climbers and wall shrubs, including *Actinidia kolomikta*, honeysuckles, parthenocissus and vines (*Vitis*), are simple to propagate by hardwood cuttings once their leaves have dropped. Take cuttings 15cm (6in) long and root them outdoors in well-drained soil (see page 117). They should be ready for planting by next autumn or early the following spring.

Climbers for trees

When choosing a climber to grow up into a tree, match the vigour of the climber to the size of the tree; a rampant climbing plant will overwhelm a small specimen. For the climber to grow successfully you need to plant and tend it with care, because it will have to compete with the roots of the tree for water and nourishment (see opposite). The planting position should not be close to the trunk but towards the edge of the branch canopy, where the soil should have fewer roots and more moisture.

For small trees: Annual climbers such as morning glory and canary creeper (*Tropaeolum peregrinum*); *Clematis alpina*, *C. macropetala*, *C. tangutica*, *C. viticella*; large-flowered clematis hybrids; Golden hop (*Humulus lupulus* 'Aureus'); rambler roses such as *Rosa* 'Emily Gray' and *R.* 'Phyllis Bide'.

For large trees: *Clematis flammula* and *C. montana*; Virginia creeper; vigorous rambler roses such as *Rosa* 'Bobbie James', *R.* 'Paul's Himalayan Musk', *R.* 'Rambling Rector' and *R.* 'Seagull'; ornamental vines; wisteria.

Layering a shrub

1 Strip the lower leaves off a young, supple stem, and then tear the bark slightly. Peg the stem down in the soil using a loop of stiff wire.

2 Cover with fine soil or fresh potting compost.

3 Bend the end of the pegged stem upwards and tie it to a vertical cane to start training the new shrub. Water well, and keep moist in dry weather.

Layering The chocolate vine (*Akebia*), trumpet vine (*Campsis*) and ornamental vines (*Vitis*) are liable to 'bleed' sap if cut when in leaf, so they are best layered in late winter when dormant.

■ **Select a long, pliable, healthy shoot** that can be bent down to touch the ground. About 30cm (12in) from the end of the stem, use a sharp knife to remove a sliver of bark from the underside, close to a leaf joint, to stimulate rooting.

■ **Peg the wounded stem to the ground** with loops of wire, cover with a layer of soil and tie the tip of the shoot to a short stake to keep it upright. Leave for at least six months before severing, after checking that it has rooted.

Looking after supports

Keep trellis and other wooden plant supports in good condition by treating them with a preservative every few years. An annual inspection of the wood during winter will show when the coating begins to deteriorate and you can take advantage of a spell of dry weather to make it good.

■ **First, clean the wood** using a wire brush to remove algal growth and stubborn patches of dirt. Then scrub it well with a stiff brush and clean water, and allow to dry. Treat any small areas of rotting wood with wood hardener.

■ **Choose a preservative paint or stain,** making sure it is non-toxic if plants are growing close by. Follow the instructions for application, and wear protective gloves and safety glasses if necessary.

■ **Check support posts,** particularly where they go into the ground as this part is the most prone to rot. If rotting has occurred, you can often repair the post by bolting the sound part to a metal spike or a concrete spur, rather than putting in a new one.

■ **Remove rust and flaking paint** from metal supports with a wire brush. Wash the structure and allow it to dry before painting.

Training a climber into a tree

1 Plant the climber at the same depth as it was growing previously, with the exception of clematis, which benefit from deep planting with 10cm (4in) of soil covering the top of the rootball.

2 Set up one or several training canes or lines of string to lead the climber into the branches and attach the climber to these using soft string.

3 Water and mulch the new climber, and make sure that it does not dry out during its first year.

Shrubs and trees

Winter is the time to prune many shrubs and trees – as well as coppicing and pollarding – and an opportunity for you to use your artistic skills to shape and train them to suit your garden. You will also need to perform routine tasks such as planting, propagating and protection.

Winter checklist

■ **Check recently planted shrubs and trees** after any high winds or hard frost. Make sure their supports and ties are secure, and refirm any plants that have lifted.

■ **Brush snow off hedges and shrubs,** as the weight can damage the dense growth of evergreens in particular.

■ **Continue planting deciduous shrubs and trees** in prepared sites if the ground is not frozen or waterlogged (see page 118).

■ **Move misplaced shrubs and trees** to more suitable sites in the garden if the soil is workable.

■ **Repair damaged hedging and fill gaps** (see page 117).

■ **Prune established shrubs and trees,** and shape young specimens.

■ **Protect the buds** of flowering cherry trees from bird damage in late winter with fleece, or use harmless deterrent sprays and bird scarers.

The dormant winter season is the best time to transplant misplaced trees and shrubs, but avoid doing this when the weather is frosty.

■ **Protect early rhododendron flower buds** against frost with fleece, and pull up any suckers that you see.

■ **Clear hedge bases,** removing fallen leaves and wind-blown debris that could harbour pests and diseases.

■ **Trim back invasive roots** where hedges grow next to borders, by plunging a spade full depth along a line about 45cm (18in) away from the hedge.

■ **Tidy shrubs** such as *Buddleja globosa* and tree peonies, which do not need regular pruning. Remove dead or diseased wood, and any live branches that spoil the shape.

■ **Prune wintersweet and witch hazel** once the plants are mature.

■ **Prepare rhododendron planting sites,** ensuring the soil pH is lower than 5.5.

■ **Take hardwood cuttings** of deciduous plants while they are leafless.

■ **Transplant suckers** to propagate new plants (see opposite).

■ **Pot up small specimens** of early flowering shrubs such as deutzia, hydrangea and viburnum. Stand them in a cool greenhouse for early blooms.

■ **Cut spindly flowering stems** from ribes, cornus, prunus, willows and viburnums, and bring indoors to flower.

■ **Paint or spray deciduous trees** that have a history of pest and disease attack while leafless, using winter wash to kill moss and overwintering insect eggs. Spread plastic sheeting to protect surrounding plants.

Propagating from suckers

Some trees and shrubs produce suckers from their own roots – these are separate shoots, growing from shallow roots or close to the base of the parent plant. You can lift these and grow them on to create new plants, ready for planting out in a year's time. Among the shrubs and trees that can be propagated this way are lilac (see right), dogwoods, kerria, sumachs and quince.

Where suckers are unwanted they should be removed (see page 146).

Transplanting a lilac sucker

1 Once you have identified the sucker, dig down to its base to make sure that it has plenty of roots of its own.

2 Cut the sucker off where it joins a main root and pot it up in a 15–20cm (6–8in) pot of soil-based potting compost (lime-free for acid-loving gaultherias). Alternatively, space several suckers 45cm (18in) apart in a nursery bed. Leave tree suckers unpruned, but cut back shrub suckers by half.

Pruning essentials

Many people find pruning intimidating, or feel that cutting off healthy growth must be counter-productive. On the contrary – judicious pruning at the right time can do much to improve the shape, flowering and fruitfulness of plants compared to those left to grow naturally.

Pruning entails the selective removal of parts of a plant for a particular reason. The main purposes of pruning are:

■ **Maintaining the health of plants** by controlling disease, which is important to keep them vigorous and attractive. Cutting out dead and diseased portions of branches, as well as removing rubbing branches, prevents further spread and disfigurement and, in the case of trees, ensures that they are safe.

■ **Training young trees and shrubs early** ensures they flower or fruit sooner. They will also develop into more attractive specimens if they are pruned in ways that emphasise a well-spaced framework of branches. Early formative pruning can correct misshapen or excessive growth.

■ **Routine annual pruning ensures balance,** encouraging a regular supply of young productive shoots while controlling more mature growth. Strongly growing plants can make a lot of leaf and stem growth at the expense of flowers, while mature specimens may stop producing new growth and only flower erratically or at the branch tips.

■ **Fewer, higher quality blooms** can be achieved by pruning, which diverts the plant's energy away from producing heavy

The correct pruning cut

Pruning cuts through the bark, which is what protects a plant from disease. The cleaner the cut, the faster the wound will dry and heal, so it is important to keep tools sharp and avoid ragged cuts and torn bark. Plants have natural defences against injury concentrated in certain places, such as in the joint where a bud or leaf grows. Cutting close to this point helps the wound to heal quickly.

Always prune just above a bud, sloping the cut to direct water away from the bud.

Where buds are in pairs on opposite sides of the stem, cut straight across, no more than 5mm (¼in) above the buds.

A correctly pruned cut will heal quickly, whereas using blunt secateurs produces a ragged cut and torn bark, which will take longer to heal.

yields of small flowers and fruits. Some shrubs and trees with handsome foliage or bark are pruned to ensure plenty of young growth with enhanced colour or shape.

■ **Healthy plants may outgrow their allotted space** if growth is not controlled, as they will continue to grow until they reach their maximum size. Hedges must be clipped to keep them in shape and the growth of shrubs and trees restricted to keep them in balance with a garden.

How pruning works

Several different hormones regulate plant activity. Those responsible for producing new growth tend to be concentrated in the top few buds of shoot tips, where they encourage stems to lengthen while suppressing the growth of buds lower down.

If you cut off these active areas of growth, the plant redirects its energies elsewhere, usually into the buds just below the pruning cut. In this way, pruning is not just the removal of excess, misplaced or unwanted growth, but also the creative and predictable redirection of new growth.

Pruning equipment

■ **A garden knife** should be used to trim young, thin growth, to tidy round large cuts, and to take cuttings.

■ **A pair of secateurs** is the essential pruning tool to cut stems up to 1cm (½in) thick. Check out the various types to find the one you prefer. Bypass secateurs are used most frequently, for most kinds of pruning.

■ **Long-handled pruners,** or loppers, are secateurs with long handles. These give greater reach and more leverage when cutting stems up to 2cm (¾in) thick.

■ **Tree pruners** are ideal for removing high branches up to 2–3cm (1in) thick. They are basically a pole, sometimes telescopic, topped with a secateur-like cutting blade.

■ **A pruning saw** is a narrow-bladed saw that is used to remove branches up to 8cm (3in) thick. Straight, curved and folding models are available, with large teeth for cutting sappy wood or smaller teeth for use on dry material.

■ **A bow saw** has a bent metal frame and a slim detachable blade; use this type of saw to cut through large tree branches.

Pruning large branches

Before cutting off a large tree branch, make sure you feel able to do the work safely. If in doubt, or if the branch is more than 20cm (8in) in diameter, consider hiring a qualified tree surgeon, especially if the branch is well above ground level. Make the final cut flush not with the trunk but with the branch collar, the swollen area where the branch and trunk join.

Removing a large branch

1 Make a preliminary upward cut, about a quarter of the way through the branch and 30–45cm (12–18in) from the trunk. Saw through the branch from above, cutting 2–3cm (1in) outside the first cut, which will close and absorb the branch's weight, making it easier to saw.

2 Saw off the remaining stub by making a small cut on the underside, close to the trunk, but not quite flush with it; finish by sawing from above to meet this cut.

Removing suckers

Suckers are shoots produced from the base or the roots of a tree or shrub, especially if the variety has been grafted on a different rootstock. They often look distinctive and grow vigorously, spoiling the shape of the plant and, if derived from a rootstock, can come to dominate the rest of the shrub. To prevent this, they should be cut out while young (see below).

Thin stems, known as water shoots, often grow on a trunk, especially around the edge of a wound left after the removal of a branch. Although these are not, strictly speaking, suckers, they too spoil the look of a plant and should be removed.

Removing suckers

1 Suckers grow vigorously and must be removed.
2 Cut off larger suckers as close to the stem or roots as possible. For the best results, scrape back the soil and pull them off at source. You can use suckers from ungrafted plants as a method of propagation (see page 143).

Keeping a tree symmetrical

Sometimes the growing tip of a tree splits to produce two or more competing main shoots (leaders). As well as spoiling the overall symmetry of the tree, these leaders usually branch at a narrow angle, creating a weak point on the tree that can later be damaged by strong winds. Some trees and shrubs, such as holly, produce vigorous new leading shoots that spoil the shape of the bush or tree if they are left to grow. These need to be cut out so a more balanced profile can develop (see below).

Remove an over-vigorous leading shoot, left, with loppers, cutting at or just below the main outline. Trim the tips of other main shoots to check their growth and encourage them to branch.
If a tree has competing main shoots (leaders), right, select the strongest shoot and cleanly cut out its rivals at their base. Check in a year or two that no shoots are growing from the pruning wounds.

Coppicing and pollarding

You can enhance the ornamental value and appearance of some trees and shrubs by using special pruning techniques.

Woody plants react to pruning by producing fresh growth. The harder they are pruned, the more vigorous their response will be, and this predictable behaviour is often exploited in hard pruning shrubs and trees, the young stems and foliage of which are more colourful or shapely than those of mature plants. Two traditional methods of hard pruning are coppicing (or stooling) and pollarding. Both of these styles are useful but they produce dramatically different effects.

■ **Coppicing shrubs** produces a large crop of new shoots of medium height and it allows a number of plants to be grown in a relatively small space. All the plant's growth is cut back regularly, usually annually, close to ground level.

■ **Pollarding** is like coppicing but leaves permanent main stems of manageable size. It allows plants to retain single or multiple main stems of a certain height, above which all growth is hard pruned.

TIP Frequent heavy pruning can lead to weakened plants, so it is important that they are fed and well mulched afterwards.

For colourful stems Hard prune coloured willows, red, green and yellow-stemmed dogwoods and the white-stemmed bramble, *Rubus cockburnianus*, in spring to stimulate plenty of young regrowth with the brightest winter colouring.

■ **Immediately after planting,** cut all stems down almost to ground level. This helps shrubs like dogwoods to form a low woody base, while the bramble responds by producing numerous young canes.

■ **Thereafter, cut stems back hard** in late winter to mid-spring.

■ **To enjoy the flowers of dogwoods** in combination with the bright young stems, coppice just half the stems and leave the others untouched. This also helps the shrub to build up strength, and can be a useful compromise if new growth has been poor.

For improved foliage Some trees produce their most handsome leaves on young stems, and coppicing is a useful technique for displaying these to advantage. Tree of heaven (*Ailanthus*), paulownia and many ornamental elders such as the golden

cut-leaved *Sambucus racemosa* 'Plumosa Aurea', all produce luxuriant foliage, often brightly coloured or of enormous size, when coppiced in spring.

The smoke bush, *Cotinus coggygria*, has fine foliage if coppiced, or attractive wispy flowers when left unpruned. Young *Eucalyptus gunnii* has rounded, blue-green juvenile leaves that are more attractive than the grey-green adult foliage. This and other eucalyptus can be coppiced or pollarded to 1–1.2m (3–4ft) high in March or April, with all growth trimmed annually to 5–8cm (2–3in) from its base.

Coppicing hazel

1 Purple hazel produces more vividly coloured foliage and useful crops of peasticks if coppiced when two to three years old.

2 Cut off all growth to ground level, leaving cuts that slope away from the centre of the plant; feed afterwards for maximum regrowth.

Hardy shrubs and seasonal flowers in tubs and window boxes keep the patio cheerful throughout the winter, but in all but the mildest areas containers will need protection from frost. Towards the end of winter, tidy up and clean patios and any other hard surfaces to prevent them from becoming slippery.

Winter checklist

■ **Move containers** that are not frost-proof under cover, to a greenhouse, conservatory or coldframe.

■ **Clean paved paths,** patios and decking (see page 42).

■ **Empty out containers** of frost-tender plants that are dead. Scrub the containers using hot water and a mild detergent, rinse and leave to dry, then store under cover.

■ **Protect container-grown plants** against frost (see right). The extent of the protection that is required will depend on the hardiness of the plant.

■ **Top-dress pot-grown lilies** while the bulbs are dormant by removing the top 10cm (4in) of old soil and replacing it with fresh, loam-based potting compost.

■ **Water occasionally** if the compost begins to dry out. Regularly check containers that are standing close to a wall and so may not receive any rainfall.

A window box planting for winter relies on colourful foliage. This one includes silver-leaved cineraria, grey-leaved senecio, variegated ivy and the winter cherry (*Solanum capsicastrum*).

Frost protection

All container-grown plants need some degree of protection from frost, because both rootball and topgrowth are above the ground. Evergreens are particularly vulnerable, as they continue to lose water through their leaves and are unable to replenish their stocks if their roots are in frozen compost. The ideal solution is to move any susceptible plants into an unheated greenhouse, porch or conservatory, but if there is no such structure available plants have to be protected outside.

Ensuring good drainage

It is vital to provide good drainage as soggy compost that freezes can result in severe damage to plants. When planting up pots, first put in a 5cm (2in) layer of drainage material, such as pieces of broken pot or chunks of polystyrene. Make sure surplus water can drain away by raising containers just off the ground, either on 'pot feet', pieces of tile, or by standing them on gravel.

Grouping containers

If severe weather threatens, move all containers against a wall, standing them shoulder to shoulder; this will raise the temperature around the pots.

■ **Wrap insulating material,** such as bubble plastic, sacking or thick wads of straw around the pots.

■ **Cover the plants** with thick horticultural fleece during very cold spells, but remove this during the day or as soon as the weather improves, otherwise fungal disease may become a problem.

■ **Remember that** well-protected plants may need watering.

Protecting plants

Standard evergreens, tree ferns and other tall plants benefit from individual protection. Remove coverings during the day unless very low temperatures persist.

Tie up the leaves (right) of cordylines, then wrap the whole plant in fleece or bubble plastic.

Insulate container-grown plants (far right) that are not fully hardy with an 'overcoat' of sacking and straw in severe weather.

Wrap the stems of standard evergreens in pipe insulation (top), then cover the pot and the head of the plant with fleece (left).

Fold the dead fronds of tree ferns over the top of the crown (top), before encasing the whole plant in a 'jacket' of bubble plastic (above).

Although we think of winter as a time when the lawn takes a rest, this really only applies when conditions are very cold. During mild spells, the grass will often grow and you can mow, repair turf, improve drainage or even make a new lawn. This is also the time to ensure your mower is ready for spring.

Winter checklist

■ **Rake up any leaves,** which if left will block out light, hold moisture and encourage moss to establish.

■ **Scatter worm casts** with a stiff broom or besom to prevent the mounds of soil being smeared by feet or by the mower and killing the grass.

■ **Make a final winter cut** with the mower blades on a high setting (see opposite). Rake off any clippings to prevent them from killing the grass beneath. During mild winters, you may need to cut the grass more than once if it continues to grow.

■ **Avoid walking over a frosted lawn** as the pressure damages the grass, causing it to turn brown and, possibly, to die.

■ **'Top' newly established lawns** with the mower blades on their highest setting to encourage more shoots from the base of the plants. If the new grass is quite low, roll it lightly to encourage branching and a denser lawn (not in frosty conditions).

■ **Apply lime to lawns on acid soil** if moss has been a particular problem.

■ **Improve drainage** by spiking with a garden fork or slitting with a scarifying machine (see right).

■ **In mild conditions** carry out minor repairs, such as mending damaged lawn edges and evening out bumps and hollows that have formed as parts of the lawn settle (see page 123).

■ **Prepare the soil for new grass** during mild weather. You can lay turf or sow seed during winter, but growth will be slow if the soil temperature drops below 5°C (40°F). In early winter, seed is the better option as turf may dry out along its edges if there are any hard frosts within the first weeks after laying.

Improving drainage

The problem that causes most damage in winter is wet, rather than cold. Long periods of mild, wet weather starve the roots of air as they are trying to grow. During the summer, lawns often develop a compacted, impervious layer just below the surface as a result of regular foot traffic, and this impedes drainage unless it is opened up by spiking or slitting.

■ **Spike with a garden fork** or, preferably, a hollow-tined lawn spiker, to help air get to the grass roots. Drive in the tines 15cm (6in) deep every 15–20cm (6–8in).

■ **Slitting with a powered scarifying machine** is an easier and quicker way to deal with a large lawn and also gathers surface debris, such as dead grass and moss. Blades cut into the top 2–3cm (1in) of soil. As well as improving lawn drainage, scarifiers prune the grass roots, encouraging them to branch.

■ **After spiking or slitting,** top-dress lawns on heavier soils with a mixture of equal

A hollow-tined lawn aerator will remove tiny plugs of soil as you push it into the lawn and thus improve the drainage.

parts of sand and loam, brushing it into the holes. This will help to improve drainage.
■ **For areas that get very wet,** you can lay land drains; do this early in winter before the ground is too wet.

Equipment overhaul

In late autumn and winter, when the grass hardly grows at all, take the opportunity to check over your mower and other lawn-care equipment. Clean electrically powered machinery, such as mowers and scarifiers (see right). Check all moving parts and then oil them, and sharpen blades with a file to regain a sharp edge, replacing any that are badly worn if necessary.
■ **Petrol-driven mowers** can be washed clean with a power hose and left to dry, but this is not recommended for machinery powered by battery or electricity.
■ **Cylinder mowers** will need to be serviced by a specialist, who will sharpen the blades on a grinding lathe.

Cleaning tip

Use a plastic scraper to clean off any caked grass stuck to the mower. This not only makes it easier to examine but also protects your mower, as grass sap stains plastic and corrodes metal. Where grass is lodged in places that are difficult to clean, blow it out with a few blasts from a bicycle pump.

Raising the blades of a rotary mower

1 Always wear a thick leather glove to grip the blade as it may be sharp. Then, using the spanner provided, slacken the spindle nut that holds the cutting blade onto the underside of the mower.

2 Carefully remove the spindle nut, the cutting blade and the spacer washer from the mower. This is a good opportunity to remove any grass cuttings that have become caked to the blade or mower.

3 Now re-attach the blade and spindle nut (but not the spacer washer – keep this safe); tighten the spindle nut. Without the spacer washer, the blade is raised and the mower will cut at a higher setting.

The greenhouse is a sanctuary for gardeners as well as for tender plants. Visit it regularly to sow, prune and check that all is well; air it on fine days and water growing plants occasionally. Forced bulbs will be coming into flower if you have provided a little warmth.

Winter checklist

■ **Water plants sparingly** in cold weather, and avoid wetting foliage (see opposite).

■ **Open ventilators** for a short period on frost-free and fog-free days to prevent the air from stagnating.

■ **Make sure heaters are working** properly, and monitor temperature levels with a maximum-minimum thermometer.

■ **Keep insulation materials** securely in place, and have newspapers, blankets or fleece handy for covering plants in extreme weather conditions, especially if the greenhouse is unheated.

■ **Remove dead flowers and leaves,** diseased plants and mildewed cuttings to keep healthy plants free from infection.

■ **Check for vine weevils** if any of your plants start to look sick or suddenly collapse (see page 155).

■ **Inspect stored bulbs and tubers** to make sure that they are still sound.

■ **Continue to bring potted bulbs in** from outdoors as they show signs of growth and flower buds (see page 134).

■ **Pot up amaryllis** and restart older bulbs (see page 135).

■ **Continue potting up lilies** if you want early flowers.

■ **Prune greenhouse climbers** and tie in any new stems (see opposite).

■ **From midwinter,** sow greenhouse flowers, such as begonias and gloxinias, and the first half-hardy annuals.

The sheltered environment of a greenhouse protects plants in the coldest weather, and offers an opportunity to force bulbs and annuals.

■ **Start begonia and gloxinia tubers** in trays for a supply of cuttings (see page 154).
■ **Sow half-hardy annuals** and early vegetables in pots or trays.
■ **Cut down greenhouse chrysanthemums** and encourage new growth from which you can take cuttings (see page 154).
■ **There is still time to** clean out the greenhouse, and wash the glass and all the equipment (see page 126).

Winter management

Special care is essential in winter to keep plants healthy. Temperature and light levels are low, and knowing how much water and air to give plants can be tricky.

Watering Only plants in active growth will need much water. To keep these evenly moist, stand pots and trays in water until the surface starts to look damp; watering from above may just moisten the surface and leave the roots dry. Take care to avoid overwatering sensitive plants, such as calceolarias and cinerarias, which can collapse suddenly if too wet. Most other plants need just enough to prevent the compost from drying out. Try to water in the mornings, so that surplus water dries before nightfall, and avoid wetting the foliage.

On fine days open top ventilators slightly for an hour or two in the morning.

Use a maximum-minimum thermometer to check temperatures, which can prove critical in winter.

Ventilation A dry atmosphere with a gentle circulation of air without cold draughts is the ideal, so open one or two top ventilators for an hour or so during the day, unless it is foggy or frosty. If possible, open vents on the side away from the wind, and close them by midday so that warmth has time to build up before sunset.

Heat Most plants benefit from temperatures above 5–7°C (40–45°F); use a thermometer to check. You can economise by gathering tender plants in a well-insulated spot and heating only this area. Germinate seeds on a windowsill or in a warm cupboard in the house, or invest in a heated propagator.

Pruning climbers

In midwinter, clear all dead flowers and leaves from climbers, and then prune them according to size and variety. Strong-growing plants such as passionflower and bougainvillea can take over a small greenhouse unless pruned hard annually.
■ **Thin the congested growth,** aiming for a balanced arrangement of main branches. Remove any weak or spindly stems, then shorten sideshoots almost to their base.
■ **Cut out one or two older branches** to allow replacement with young, more vigorous shoots. Sort the prunings for potential cuttings before discarding them.

■ **Check the plant is symmetrical** and well shaped, with plenty of light reaching all the stems.

■ **Clean the glass or wall** behind the climber, prick over and weed the soil, and mulch plants growing in the ground.

Tuberous-rooted plants

Winter is the time for encouraging tuberous-rooted plants, such as begonias, dahlias and gloxinias, to begin to grow. This ensures they will make large flowering plants later on in the year. This is also a way to provide early shoots from which you can take cuttings (see right).

Chrysanthemums

When greenhouse and slightly tender border chrysanthemums finish flowering, cut down their topgrowth to 5–8cm (2–3in) high. Overwinter them in a cool, frost-free place: indoor varieties in their pots, border kinds dug up and packed in soil in a coldframe or under the greenhouse staging. Keep watering to a minimum, supplying just enough to prevent the plants from drying out. New shoots will appear from late December onwards, depending on the variety. Use these for cuttings when they are about 8cm (3in) long.

■ **Cut off all the lower leaves** and trim each cutting just below a leaf joint.

■ **Insert them 2–3cm (1in) deep** in pots of cuttings compost mixed with added sharp sand; five will fit comfortably into a 15cm (6in) pot.

■ **Water the cuttings,** cover the pots with a clear plastic bag and keep in a light, warm position until rooted.

Alpines

Winter is the ideal time to sow the seeds of many alpines as they require a period of cold, known as stratification, in order to germinate. Sedums, campanulas, saxifrages, dianthus and scutellaria are all suitable for sowing in the greenhouse now.

Starting begonias into growth

1 Fill a tray with moist potting compost and press tubers into this, 5cm (2in) apart, so their tops are just above surface level. Make sure they are the right way up, with the rounded base downwards and the hollowed area uppermost, then water them.

2 Cut very large tubers in half with a sharp knife to increase the number of plants, but dust the cut edges with yellow sulphur powder as a precaution against rotting. Use a propagator or cover the tray with a clear lid and keep moist at 13–15°C (55–60°F). In a cooler greenhouse, delay planting until early spring.

3 When growth appears, pot up the tubers individually.

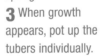

Sowing the seeds of alpines

1 Mix up a growing medium of equal parts seed-and-cuttings compost and perlite or sharp sand. Fill pots and water gently. Spread the seeds thinly and evenly over the surface.

2 Cover seeds to their own depth with sieved compost and top with a 1cm (½in) layer of grit to protect the seeds and prevent moss growing. For fine seeds, cover only with grit.

3 Once seedlings start to show through, prick out those with two true leaves and pot on; grow on in the coldframe. Return the first pot to the coldframe to allow other seeds to germinate.

To give alpines the sharp drainage they need, mix a special potting compost of equal parts by volume of seed-and-cuttings compost and perlite or sharp sand. Water the compost before you sow in order to avoid washing the seeds deep down into the growing medium where they will not germinate. After sowing, stand the pots in a coldframe; alpines are not tender but they need protection from winter wet.

The seedlings may take several months to show throught the grit. Prick them out carefully once two true leaves have formed, then put the pot back in the coldframe to encourage more seeds to germinate. This process can take up to a year.

Vine weevils

The damaging effects of this troublesome weevil, the grubs of which feed on roots, can be obvious in winter. If plants start to look sick and then suddenly collapse, tip them out carefully and explore the compost for the curved larvae, which are creamy white with brown heads.

■ **Inspect plants** in the evening for irregular holes round the edges of leaves – typical evidence of adults feeding – and crush any weevils that you find.

■ **Use a biological control** during summer when the temperature is at least 12°C (54°F). Water any affected plants with a parasitic nematode (Heterorhabditis), which will kill the weevil grubs.

■ **Throughout the year**, tip out plants occasionally to check for grubs and inspect new plants before introducing them to the greenhouse.

■ **Surround the rims** of precious plants with double-sided sticky tape to trap adults before they can lay eggs.

■ **To prevent an attack** by vine weevils, try using an insecticidal compost that contains imidocloprid.

160 Acknowledgments

© RD = Reader's Digest Association, All artwork=© Reader's Digest Association

T=Top, B=Bottom, L=Left, R=Right, C=Centre

Front Cover Gap Photos Ltd/ Zara Napier
1 The Garden Collection/Marie O'Hara, **2-3** The Garden Collection/Liz Eddision/Design: Chris Beardshaw, **4 T** ShutterStock, Inc/Hannamariah, **B** The Garden Collection/Andrew Lawson, **5 T** Garden World Images/Lee Thomas, **B** ShutterStock, Inc/Radim Strojek, **6** The Garden Collection/Andrew Lawson, **8-9** ShutterStock, Inc/Cheryl Casey, **10** Garden World Images, **11** © Reader's Digest/Mark Winwood, **12** © Reader's Digest/Sarah Cuttle, **13 TL, TC, TR** © Reader's Digest/Mark Winwood, **13 B, 14** © Reader's Digest/Sarah Cuttle, **15** © Reader's Digest/Mike Newton, **16** © Reader's Digest/Mark Winwood, **17** © Reader's Digest/Sarah Cuttle, **18** © Reader's Digest/Mark Winwood, **19** Andrew Lawson, **21 TL, TC, TR** © Reader's Digest/Mark Winwood, **B** Andrew Lawson, **22-23** © Reader's Digest/Mark Winwood, **24, 25 TL, TR, CR** © Reader's Digest/Sarah Cuttle, **25 B, 26-29 T** © Reader's Digest/Mark Winwood, **29 L, CL, CR, BR** © Reader's Digest/Sarah Cuttle, **30-31** © Reader's Digest/Mark Winwood, **32** © Reader's Digest/Sarah Cuttle, **33** © Reader's Digest/Mark Winwood, **34** ShutterStock, Inc/Wiz Data, Inc., **35** © Reader's Digest, **36-39** © Reader's Digest/Mark Winwood, **40-42** © Reader's Digest/Sarah Cuttle, **43** © Reader's Digest/Debbie Patterson, **44, 45 T, C** © Reader's Digest/Sarah Cuttle, **B** © Reader's Digest/Mike Newton, **46-51** © Reader's Digest/Mark Winwood, **52** Photolibrary Group/P Windsor, **53 L, CL, C, CR, R** © Reader's Digest/Mark Winwood, **B** © Reader's Digest/Sarah Cuttle, **54, 55 T** © Reader's Digest/Mark Winwood, **R** iStockphoto.com/Jeff Gynane, **56-57** ShutterStock, Inc/Vera Bogaerts, **58** iStockphoto.com/Michael Cook, **59-63** © Reader's Digest/ Mark Winwood, **64** © Reader's Digest/Maddie Thornhill, **65-66** © Reader's Digest/Sarah Cuttle, **67** © Reader's Digest/Maddie Thornhill, **68** © Reader's Digest, **69-70** © Reader's Digest/Mark Winwood, **71 T** © Reader's Digest/Sarah Cuttle, **B** © Reader's Digest/Mark Winwood, **72** Photolibrary Group/Eric Crichton, **73** © Reader's Digest/Sarah Cuttle, **74-75** © Reader's Digest/Mark Winwood, **76** Clive Nichols, **77 TL, TC** © Reader's Digest/Sarah Cuttle, **77 B, 78** © Reader's Digest/Mark Winwood, **79 T** Justyn Willsmore, **B** Getty Images Ltd/Dorling Kindersley, **80** Gap Photos Ltd/Howard Rice, **81** © Reader's Digest/Sarah Cuttle, **82** © Reader's Digest/Mark Winwood, **83** © Reader's Digest, **84-87** © Reader's Digest/Mark Winwood, **89** Andrew Lawson, **90** © Reader's Digest/Sarah Cuttle, **91 T** Photolibrary Group/J. Glover, **BL, BR** © Reader's Digest/Sarah Cuttle, **92 L** Photolibrary Group/G. Glynn-Smith, **R** Photolibrary Group/J. Sorrell, **93** © Reader's Digest/M. Newton, **94** © Reader's Digest/Mark Winwood, **95** ShutterStock, Inc/Catherine Jones, **96-97** © Reader's Digest/Mark Winwood, **98** © Reader's Digest/Debbie Patterson, **99-101** © Reader's Digest/Mark Winwood, **102** Mark Winwood, **103** © Reader's Digest/Mark Winwood, **104-105** ShutterStock, Inc/Andrejs Pidjass, **106** © Reader's Digest/Mark Winwood, **107** © Reader's Digest/Mark Winwood, **108** iStockphoto.com, **109 TL, TR** © Reader's Digest/Sarah Cuttle, **BL, BR** © Reader's Digest/Mark Winwood, **110** iStockphoto.com/Kjell Brynildsen, **111-115** © Reader's Digest/Mark Winwood, **116** Photolibrary Group/Mark Bolton, **117** © Reader's Digest/Sarah Cuttle, **118** © Reader's Digest/Mark Winwood, **119 TR, CR, BR** © Reader's Digest/Sarah Cuttle, **TL, CLT, CLB, BL** © Reader's Digest/Mark Winwood, **120** © Reader's Digest/Mark Winwood, **121 T, BL, BC** © Reader's Digest/Sarah Cuttle, **121 BR, 122-123** © Reader's Digest/Mark Winwood **124** © Reader's Digest/Debbie Patterson, **125** Garden World Images/T. McGlinchey, **126-127** © Reader's Digest/Mark Winwood, **128-129** ShutterStock, Inc/Lijuan Guo, **130** iStockphoto.com, **131** © Reader's Digest/Mark Winwood, **132** © Reader's Digest/Debbie Patterson, **133 T, C, B** © Reader's Digest/Mark Winwood, **BL** © Reader's Digest/Maddie Thornhill, **134-135** © Reader's Digest/Sarah Cuttle, **136** Photolibrary Group/H. Rice, **137** © Reader's Digest/Sarah Cuttle, **138** Photolibrary Group/J. Glover, **139** © Reader's Digest/Mark Winwood, **140** © Reader's Digest/Sarah Cuttle, **141** © Reader's Digest/Mark Winwood, **142** Photolibrary Group/M O'Hara, **143** © Reader's Digest/Mark Winwood, **144** © Reader's Digest/Sarah Cuttle, **145** © Reader's Digest/Mark Winwood, **146 TL,TR, BL** © Reader's Digest/Mark Winwood, **146 C, 147** © Reader's Digest/Sarah Cuttle, **148** Photolibrary Group/L. Brotchie, **149** © Reader's Digest/Sarah Cuttle, **150-151** © Reader's Digest/Mark Winwood, **152** Photolibrary Group/Mayer Le Scanff, **153-154** © Reader's Digest/Mark Winwood, **155** © Reader's Digest/Sarah Cuttle

Reader's Digest Year-round Gardening is based on material in *The Complete Guide to Gardening Season by Season*, published by The Reader's Digest Association Limited, London.

First Edition Copyright © 2008

The Reader's Digest Association Limited, 11 Westferry Circus, Canary Wharf, London E14 4HE www.readersdigest.co.uk

Editors Caroline Smith, Diane Cross
Art Editors Louise Turpin, Julie Bennett
Proofreader Rosemary Wighton
Indexer Hilary Bird
Picture Researcher Rosie Taylor

Reader's Digest General Books
Editorial Director Julian Browne
Art Director Anne-Marie Bulat
Managing Editor Nina Hathway
Head of Book Development Sarah Bloxham
Picture Resource Manager Sarah Stewart-Richardson
Pre-press Account Manager Dean Russell
Production Controller Sandra Fuller
Product Production Manager Claudette Bramble

Origination Colour Systems Limited, London
Printed in China

All rights reserved.

No part of this book may be reproduced, stored in a retrieval system or transmitted in any form or by any means, electronic, electrostatic, magnetic tape, mechanical, photocopying, recording or otherwise, without permission in writing from the publishers.

® Reader's Digest, The Digest and the Pegasus logo are registered trademarks of The Reader's Digest Association, Inc., of Pleasantville, New York, USA

We are committed both to the quality of our products and the service we provide to our customers. We value your comments, so please do contact us on **08705 113366** or via our website at **www.readersdigest.co.uk**

If you have any comments or suggestions about the content of our books, email us at **gbeditorial@readersdigest.co.uk**

ISBN 978 0 276 44378 7
BOOK CODE 400-381 UP0000-1
ORACLE CODE 250012534H.00.24